The Language of Jazz

Also from Carcanet

Fly-fishing: a book of words
C. B. McCully

Horse Racing: a book of words
Gerald Hammond

Theatre: a book of words
Martin Harrison

Whisky: a book of words
Gavin D. Smith

The Language of Cricket
John Eddowes

The Language of the Field
Michael Brander

Neil Powell

The Language of Jazz

CARCANET

First published in Great Britain in 1997 by
Carcanet Press Limited
4th floor, Conavon Court
12–16 Blackfriars Street
Manchester M3 5BQ

A CIP catalogue record for this book
is available from the British Library.
ISBN 1 85754 164 2

The publisher acknowledges financial
assistance from the Arts Council of England.

Set in 10pt Plantin by XL Publishing Services, Tiverton
printed and bound in England by SRP Ltd, Exeter

For Peter Thornton (about time too),
Seamus Murphy, and Adam Oliver

General Editors' Preface

This series offers a new conception and analysis of the vocabularies used in our sports, pursuits, vocations and pastimes. While each book contains an essential lexicon of words and phrases – explored historically and in depth – each also contains generous quotation, practical reference, anecdote and conjecture. The result is more than a dictionary: specific, inclusive, thought-provoking, each volume offers the past and present through a weave of words, in all their curiosity and delight.

Those intrigued by the language particular to their area of interest will find the relevant book a coherent and challenging treatment of the topic; those interested in the English language itself will find the series yielding significant material on semantic scope and change; and general readers who wish to understand the vocabularies of human endeavour will find the series tracing the necessary but implacable relationships between words and world.

Editors, chosen because of their intimate enthusiasm for their subjects, have been encouraged to be comprehensive in their coverage: vocabularies typically range from the demotic to the esoteric, from slang to the technical and specialised. Within that range, emphasis is also placed on *how* each lexicon developed, and why its terms acquired their peculiar descriptive power. These are books to read with pleasure as well as keep on the reference shelf.

Gerald Hammond
C. B. McCully

A Four-Bar Intro

1

The word 'jazz', as the historian Eric Hobsbawm (writing in his jazz-critic disguise of Francis Newton) once pointed out, only 'entered print and printable meaning' in about 1915. It shares with its quarrelsome near-contemporary sibling, cinema, the distinction of being an art-form almost exactly of the twentieth century: born into the modern world, defined by and defining its epoch, subject to irrevocable and quite possibly terminal change as the millennium closes. It is like cinema, too, in seeming to be the new world's gift to the old: if film is synonymous in the public imagination with Hollywood, jazz is as inextricably linked with New Orleans; of all the western arts, these two speak most characteristically in the accents of America.

'I invented jazz in 1902,' claimed Jelly Roll Morton. He was in the right place at the right time – New Orleans at the turn of the century – and his claim is as good as anyone else's. But it would be truer to say that jazz (as distinct from its related precursors such as blues or ragtime) originated in a somewhat unlikely fusion of two elements within the city of New Orleans. The first of these was a particular group of citizens, the Creoles or *gens de couleur*, who more than any others embodied the complex cultural history of the place: its French foundation in 1718, Spanish governance from 1764 to 1800, and brief return to French control before Napoleon sold it to the United States in 1803. Creole music owed a great deal to the elegant, rather stately forms of the French tradition: 'The instrumentation of early New Orleans jazz, which is essentially that of the military band, the instrumental technique, particularly obvious in that French speciality, the woodwind, the repertoire of marches, quadrilles, waltzes, and the like – all are unmistakably French' (Newton, 31). Nevertheless, the marching bands did not play music which we would generally recognise as jazz, and they might have marched on into obscurity had it not been for a second, and apparently unrelated, development within New Orleans towards the end of the nineteenth century. This was the opening in 1897 of the official red-light district, subsequently known (after the virtuous alderman who created it) as Storyville, and the demand for a quite different kind of musician in its cabarets, brothels, barrel-houses and gambling-joints: the solo pianist, often of great technical accomplishment and with a repertoire which might typically range from versions of European classical music through ragtime to blues. When this solo pianist augmented himself with bass or guitar or banjo and drums he turned himself into a rhythm section; and when that rhythm section teamed up with the now-stationary brass and woodwinds, the distinctively hybrid ensemble universally recognised as a jazz band was born.

Jazz is easy to recognise but treacherously difficult to analyse: it both invites and repels exegesis. It has close affinities with poetry: not so much in the genially blurred way suggested by the poetry-and-jazz movement of the late 1950s as in its ability constantly to renew and to re-invent certain given forms. Just as the sonnet and the iambic lyric have proved mysteriously inexhaustible to writers, so the parallel forms of the twelve-bar blues and the 32-bar AABA standard song have shaped and sustained a far greater and more complex range of music than should seem logically or mathematically feasible; some indication of how this occurs is provided within the entries for *blues* and *standard*. But these forms, though central to jazz, will not in themselves define it: a blues when performed by Elvis Presley becomes rock 'n' roll; a standard song when sung by Tony Bennett is mere middle-of-the-road pop. At almost every point in jazz's short history, a lively and indeed excitable debate has raged about where these border-lines should be drawn, usually focusing less on instrumentalists – who have often doubled as session musicians for film sound-tracks, dance bands or pop backing groups to make ends meet – than on high-profile vocalists. For years Ella Fitzgerald was sneeringly dismissed in the jazz press as a commercial pop singer, especially after she made her famous series of 'Songbook' albums in the 1950s, their success doubtless being at least half the problem; while Frank Sinatra, white and male as well as immoderately popular, has never been fully admitted to the fold, despite that momentous recording date with Count Basie (of which Sinatra said, 'I've waited twenty years for this moment') in October 1962.

Yet time has, I think, taught us to be more indulgent than we once were towards the cross-fertilisations of the dance-band era. Firstly, it was the enriched instrumentation of popular dance music – and specifically its use of saxophones – which allowed jazz bandleaders like Duke Ellington and Fletcher Henderson to move beyond the inimitable but limited music of the New Orleans tradition. Secondly, the finest jazz musicians of the 1930s and 1940s, especially British ones, very often worked within dance bands, their brief solos miraculously flowering out of relatively pedestrian arrangements; while in some cases dance-band composers and arrangers themselves produced scores of startling originality (an example which became familiar half a century later, when it was used in Dennis Potter's *Pennies from Heaven*, is Reginald Forsythe's 'Garden of Weed', recorded by Lew Stone and his Band for Decca in 1934). And thirdly, much of the musical material was interchangeable: every jazz band played Cole Porter's 'Night and Day', while every dance band played Ellington's 'Solitude'.

This homogeneity was, however, disrupted in the early 1950s by the arrival of rock 'n' roll which, despite its common ancestry via rhythm and blues, was essentially inimical to jazz: not only was it far less subtle rhythmically, with its heavily accented on-beat and its lack of syncopation; it also relied predominantly on the electric guitar, an instrument which has never made much sense to jazz musicians, rather than on the brass and reeds of the familiar front line (whose vestigial remains nevertheless surfaced in an occasional snarling or bawling sax). As jazz largely severed its mutually nourishing links with the popular mainstream, it became more eclectic and experimental: characteristic post-war movements such as bebop, cool, third stream and other segments of the avant-garde depend precisely on the fact that their performers are *not* earning their bread and butter behind the orchestra desks of Tommy Dorsey or Glenn Miller, Bert Ambrose or Harry Roy. And this change in the music's status naturally coincided with a change in its audience: though jazz had always been attractive to students (as in the well-documented cases of Philip Larkin and Kingsley Amis at Oxford), it was in the 1950s that it became both a symbol of intellectual rebellion – in, for instance, John Osborne's *Look Back in Anger* – and a subject of furious factional argument.

For the years in which post-war 'modern' jazz developed and flourished in its own impressive diversity – not only Charlie Parker, Dizzy Gillespie and Thelonious Monk, but also Lester Young, Bud Powell, Miles Davis, Sonny Rollins, Gerry Mulligan, the MJQ and so many others – were also marked by a consider-able interest in revivalist New Orleans and Dixieland jazz, an interest which in Britain led directly to the wildly anachronistic popularity of 'trad' during the early 1960s. The two factions are easily caricatured: neat, cerebral modernists, reading Sartre and

drinking Pernod; hearty, bearded *Manchester Guardian*-reading
and ale-swilling revivalists – the cool and the hot, in fact: the
recurring polarity in post-war popular culture, which re-emerged
a little later in the exactly parallel contrasts between 'mods' and
'rockers'. If a heretical jazz musician shifted his ground from the
New Orleans revival into the mainstream, as Humphrey Lyttelton
did in 1953 when he introduced that impure object the saxophone (and with it Bruce Turner) into his band, he could be sure
of provoking rage and lamentation of theological intensity from
his purist audience. The revivalist movement's British 'trad' tail-
end – exemplified by the extraordinary hit records of Acker Bilk,
Kenny Ball, The Temperance Seven – was obviously no more
than an exercise in nostalgic kitsch, distant in terms both of
musical quality and of emotional authenticity from the world of
Armstrong, Bechet and Morton to which it paid homage; yet the
very persistence of that nostalgic impulse clearly indicates the
enduring attraction of New Orleans jazz. As it happens, the same
period also contains striking evidence of the way in which quite
other forms of jazz might unexpectedly reappear in the world of
pop music: the astonishing successes of the Dave Brubeck
Quartet's 'Take Five' in 1961 and, two years later, of 'Desafinado'
and other bossa nova pieces by Stan Getz, Charlie Byrd and
Astrud Gilberto. Just when you think jazz has retrenched irre-
versibly into a minority niche, isolated from the popular
mainstream, it re-emerges in the pop charts or film scores or TV
commercials: Louis Armstrong died in 1971, yet his inimitable
voice was eerily persuading people to drink draught Guinness
(and still selling records) in 1995. How right Whitney Balliett
was to call his first collection of essays on jazz *The Sound of
Surprise*.

2

The history of jazz runs exactly in parallel with the history of the
gramophone record. Both were inventions of the late nineteenth
century; after that, the balance of cause and effect is endlessly
debatable, but what is beyond dispute is jazz's plain good luck.
'The year 1923,' says Humphrey Lyttelton, 'is to jazz history what
1066 is to the schoolboy's table of dates. In that year, King
Oliver's Creole Jazz Band made the batch of recordings which
are generally taken as the starting-point in the development of
jazz on record' (Lyttelton [1], 160). The introduction of electric
recording – the replacement of the acoustic horn by the micro-

phone – in 1926 coincided with the peak of the Louis Armstrong Hot Five and Seven and with the arrival in the studios of Duke Ellington's first mature orchestra. Similarly, the launch of the microgroove LP in the late 1940s occurred at the very moment when the post-bebop generation was starting to break free from the constraints of the blues and the standard popular song. This dovetailing of musical and technological evolution looks pleasingly neat, but it is not, of course, utterly infallible: there were doubtless many early unrecorded musicians (like the legendary Buddy Bolden) of considerable talent, while jazz composers as diverse as James P. Johnson, George Gershwin and Duke Ellington had ambitions of symphonic scale long before the invention of the LP which could have accommodated them. Nevertheless, with jazz we have a unique record – in both senses – of an art-form evolving in performance, and this is very nearly an unmixed blessing: the one danger is that the wealth of documentation may have an inhibiting or truncating effect, rather as if, through some perverse technological miracle, a theatre director were to be confronted with videotapes of Shakepeare's own productions or a musician with Bach's own performances in digital stereo. Because jazz is an art in which everyone has access to the old masters, it is a cruel one for even the most gifted of imitators.

Given this abundant aural evidence, it seems extraordinary that jazz has been so widely (and, one suspects, wilfully) misunderstood: many white European listeners seem to have until quite recently believed it to be a primitive, cacophonous sort of black American folk music, altogether disreputable, and indistinguishable from 'ragtime' or 'blues' – an ironic misconception since French and Spanish influences were so vital to the origins of New Orleans jazz. The most extreme, and apparently most authoritative, instance of such misunderstanding was probably the five-page entry for 'Jazz' in Percy A. Scholes' *Oxford Companion to Music* (I am referring to the ninth edition of 1955, which was still in print when I acquired my copy almost a decade later), an essay entirely constructed of malice, racism and simple ignorance (Scholes, 534–9); it is cited, briefly, elsewhere in these pages. But similar attitudes were commonplace among other people who should have known better. The novelist L.P. Hartley, for example, apparently thought that the twentieth century's cultural decline was caused by 'jazz, and the indifference to sense, and morality, and genuine emotion that goes with jazz, which in any case has to be sung slightly out of tune' (Adrian Wright, *Foreign Country*, 9). Eleanor Farjeon, in a loathsome little poem

called 'Jazz-man', assumed the term to be synonymous with a
comic one-man-band – 'Toot and Tingle! Hoot and Jingle! / Oh,
what a clatter! how the tunes all mingle!' – but what can Britten
have been thinking of when he set it to music (Boris Ford,
Benjamin Britten's Poets, 40)? And as recently as March 1995,
Donald Baverstock's obituarist in the *Independent* could try on
the old *faux-naïf* trick of using 'jazz' to mean popular-rubbish-
in-general: 'Thus, in February 1957, *Tonight* began, from 6.05
to 6.45 from Monday to Friday, with the jazz programme *Six
Five Special* filling the space on Saturday' (*Independent*, 18 March
1995).

These three instances of misrepresentation are quoted here
because they are characteristic of once widely-held attitudes, and
because they would be unwelcome in the main body of this book:
references there are, as far as possible, to writers who have had
something useful and interesting to say on the subject.

3

Like many people born after the Second World War – when the
music's hectic formative years were long passed – I stumbled over
jazz quite by chance in childhood. By the mid-1950s, once the
vinyl LP and the lightweight pick-up had become established,
people were cheerfully turfing out of their attics and into village
jumble-sales old wind-up gramophones and stacks of assorted 78
rpm records. That is how I came to possess, at the age of seven
or eight and among much miscellaneous dross, a battered copy
of Parlophone R618 – the original British issue of 'St Louis Blues'
by Louis Armstrong and his Orchestra, recorded in 1929. Of
course, I'd never heard of Armstrong and I had no idea what sort
of noise would emerge from the disc: the force of that revelation
– the absolutely certain sense, without any background knowledge or information, that this was something unique and
important – isn't easy to convey. It's a track which, even now,
I'd put among those to recommend to listeners coming afresh to
jazz, not perhaps with an educated ear accustomed to European
classical music but with the less sophisticated expectations of
pop. For a child, it was perfect. It drives, swings, re-invents itself,
rollicking through its final choruses with an exuberance which
leaves most 1950s rock 'n' roll sounding dull and lumpish.

What I couldn't know until much later was that this very track
was also a talisman for an older jazz fan called Philip Larkin. In
a *Daily Telegraph* review first published in 1968, Larkin described

'St Louis Blues' as 'the hottest record ever made': 'Starting *in media res*, with eight bars of the lolloping tangana release, it soon resolves into genial uptempo polyphony ... Armstrong shouts a couple of blues choruses not to be found in the original Handy song sheet, then after 12 bars of Higgie's trombone Louis leads the ensemble in four blistering choruses of solid riffing. By the third chorus the whole building seems to be moving' (Larkin, 230). Like so much of Larkin's writing on jazz, that seems both accurate and evocative – and close to unchallengable. But later still I picked up an old copy of Rex Harris's 1952 Pelican *Jazz*, a brilliantly opinionated (and often stimulatingly wrong-headed) book by a deeply committed New Orleans purist: a man very much of Larkin's tastes, I'd have thought. Here he is on the same recording: 'Of "St Louis Blues" (Parlophone R618) the less said the better, for this old traditional tune, which was "composed" by Handy, sinks towards the end into a pit of repeated riffs which even Armstrong can do nothing to save' (Harris, 119).

Jazz, then, is always a subjective business, and anyone who pretends otherwise is a bore or a fraud. Harris thought swing had been the death of jazz; Larkin that Charlie Parker – or perhaps John Coltrane or Ornette Coleman – more or less finished it off. They were both wrong, of course, but the habit is catching. For the purposes of this book, the great age of jazz probably covers around fifty years – say from the 1920s to the 1970s: before it is an important evolutionary period; after it, jazz begins to merge inextricably with other kinds of music. This last assertion may well look ridiculous in time; I let it stand, however, because a book like this one shouldn't attempt to deal fully with the immediate past, in which terms and usages are still treacherously fluid, and because the rough frame I propose does embrace the central careers of all the undeniably major jazz performers and composers. Jazz is flourishing in the 1990s and it will doubtless continue to flourish; but its historical moment was beginning to wane twenty years ago, and if it eventually evolves into something with another name we shouldn't mourn it. My own guess is that 'jazz' will eventually be attached to a major musical style of the mid-twentieth century very much as 'baroque' is attached to one of the late seventeenth or early eighteenth.

4

The Language of Jazz, like earlier volumes in this series (many of which appeared under the title *A Book of Words*), does not claim to be a comprehensive dictionary or encyclopaedia of the subject: these exist already, in any case. It is something altogether more personal, quirky and – I hope – enjoyable for anyone who loves jazz or words or both. Its entries, which are unashamedly selective, are roughly of the following types:

1. Ordinary words with special meanings in jazz: for instance, *cool, jam, stride.*
2. Words unique to jazz: *bebop, Dixieland, ragtime.*
3. Musical terms adopted by jazz: *bar, rhythm, swing.*
4. Musical instruments particularly associated with jazz: *alto, clarinet, trombone.*
5. Names and nicknames of outstanding jazz musicians: *Bird, Duke, Satchmo.*
6. Place-names associated with movements in jazz: *Chicago, Harlem, Storyville.*
7. Specialist jazz record labels: *Dial, Okeh, Savoy.*
8. Notable jazz venues: *Birdland, Cotton Club, Minton's.*

A quick flick through the following pages will, however, indicate that these are merely the simplest of examples and that plenty of jazz words spill over into several of these categories and beyond them. For examples of usage, I am particularly indebted to two indispensable collections of jazz musicians' own recollections: *Hear Me Talkin' to Ya*, edited by Nat Shapiro and Net Hentoff, and *Swing to Bop*, edited by Ira Gitler; I have also thoroughly raided the shelf of jazz books listed in the Bibliography and, beyond these, a further range of literary sources, as well as magazine and newspaper cuttings, which are noted in the course of the text.

Some readers may find the prominence given to recorded jazz irksome but this is partly, as I've suggested above, the nature of the subject and partly the inescapable consequence of my own age and nationality. 'My' instrument, to the extent that I play one at all, is the piano, so I'm glad that I did hear Duke Ellington and Thelonious Monk when they came to London; Ella Fitzgerald, too, but not, obviously and alas, Billie Holiday; nor could I have heard Charlie Parker except on disc – while my younger self would have been snooty about the latter years of Louis Armstrong, whom I *could* have heard. However, as the discographical note at the end of the Bibliography briefly suggests, the practicalities of jazz on record are anything but straightforward: if the works of T. S. Eliot had been as randomly in and out of print, and from as many different publishers, as the works of Charlie Parker, there'd have been civil disturbances in bookshops. The best that can be said of this is that it adds to the fun of jazz record collectors, who are an exceptionally tenacious bunch of what Les Murray, describing any group of dedicated and slightly batty enthusiasts, has happily named 'groovers'.

The record companies often seem careless or cavalier; the BBC, on the other hand, obstructive and neglectful in its treatment of jazz for as long as I can remember, is guilty of an altogether more serious offence. At the time of writing, its regular jazz output consists of *Jazz Record Requests* (Radio 3, Saturdays), *The Best of Jazz* (Radio 2, Mondays), an after-midnight weekday half-hour shunted from Radio 2 to Radio 3, an immensely variable strand of thematic programmes broadcast at the eccentric time of 4.30 on Monday afternoons, and a late-night Saturday double-bill of new jazz followed by a re-run of an old Monday afternoon series – this graveyard slot effectively excluding both the sociable and the sleepy. Quite apart from its injustice to past and present musicians, this haphazard programming means that the acknowledged masterpieces of jazz probably remain unheard (and even unheard-of) by millions of listeners too young to have picked up the jazz-junkshop habit: one urgent need is consequently for some properly informed and extended broadcast series – *The Complete Armstrong Hot Fives and Sevens*, say, or *The Ellington Orchestras* or *The Parker Dials and Savoys*. Though it won't do to be too po-faced about this – and there is certainly something grotesque and deeply humourless about the academisation of jazz studies in some American universities, with their deadly earnest scholarly theses inexorably stacking up – the case might be gently stated for Armstrong's, Ellington's and Parker's music as parts of twentieth-century culture which ought to have reached everyone's ears by now.

On Saturday 15 June 1996, while I was working on this book, two distinct but relevant events occurred. In the centre of Manchester, an IRA bomb exploded, seriously damaging the Corn Exchange and leaving Carcanet Press temporarily homeless: only very temporarily, thanks to the energetic and devoted efforts of Carcanet's staff. And on the same day in Los Angeles, Ella Fitzgerald died at the age of 79. I had already written the entry for **Ella** and I haven't altered it, except to add the simple fact of her death. She was the last surviving member of that select group – including Louis Armstrong, Duke Ellington, Charlie Parker, Billie Holiday – who shaped and defined jazz not only for its own committed listeners but for a vast international audience,

to whom she gave incomparable pleasure. As Prospero says: 'Our
revels now are ended.' But what revels they were.

Neil Powell
Aldeburgh, 1997

Aeolian Hall   A highly respectable New York musical venue, the Aeolian Hall was the scene on 12 February 1924 of 'the first jazz concert that captured the imagination of an influential part of the American public' (Stearns, 120), at which Paul Whiteman and his orchestra performed works ranging from 'Livery Stable Blues' to the première of Gershwin's *Rhapsody in Blue*. Although hardly anyone since has had a good word to say for this event in particular or for his concept of 'symphonic jazz' in general, Whiteman deserves some credit for extending the jazz audience and for presenting to the public Gershwin's *Rhapsody*, 'a very reputable piece of jazz-influenced light music' (Newton, 52).

aficionado   This Spanish word, in its sense of 'a knowledgeable amateur enthusiast', acquired a particular jazz context through frequent use by *Gramophone* jazz reviewers (and prolific sleevenote writers) Charles Fox and Alun Morgan: cf. *cat*. Jim Goldbolt mentions 'the jazz aficionado's concern, obsession, even, with personnel identification' (Godbolt, 25).

air-check   An *air-check* or *air-shot* is a recording, often amateur or unauthorised, of a broadcast performance, which may be especially valuable to collectors if it combines musicians contracted to different record companies (and thus not normally heard together on disc) or if it has some particular historical importance: 'Airchecks (off-the-air recordings) from the 1930s and 1940s are always of interest since we can hear jazz musicians trying and sometimes failing to get their message across' (Clarke, 69).

alligator   A musician out to gain ideas and expertise by sitting in with an established band: 'We'd call them alligators. That was our tip-off word, because they were guys who came to swallow everything we had to learn' (Buster Bailey, quoted in Shapiro, 102). But according to a 1939 'Vocabulary of Swing Terms', an *alligator* was also 'a swing fan who plays no instrument' (*PBJ*, 134); this was to become the dominant usage in pseudo-*hip* jargon, giving rise to the 1950s phrase, tiresomely immortalised by Bill Haley, 'See you later, alligator.'

alto   The alto saxophone, like its slightly larger relative the *tenor*, is often supposed to be the quintessential jazz instrument – an impression cheerfully reinforced by innumerable graphic designers who have been unable to resist using its 'j' shape as the initial letter of the word 'jazz' – yet, as Joachim Berendt notes, 'the saxophone played scarcely any role in the jazz of the twenties – just at the time when everyone who heard a saxophone thought he was hearing jazz' (Berendt, 151). In *New Orleans* jazz, if saxophones appeared at all they were regarded as curious anachronisms, a stance rather comically mimicked later on by some post-war revivalists. Yet the saxophone had already established its place in American music during jazz's pre-history: Frank Tirro usefully reminds us that in 1876 the band of Patrick Sarsfield Gilmore comprised 66 players (35 reeds, 27 brass and four percussion) and that 'among the reeds we find all four of the saxophone family – soprano, alto, tenor, and baritone' (Tirro, 12).

The alto saxophone's achievement of its central position in jazz was among the benefits of the cross-fertilisation with popular dance music which took place during the 1920s: no orchestra was more influential in this context than *Duke* Ellington's, and in the hands of Johnny Hodges, who joined the band in 1928, the alto was the most liquidly evocative of instruments. For Charlie Parker, two decades later, the alto became the hard-edged, often astringent voice of *bebop*, while at the end of the 1950s it was the vehicle for Ornette Coleman's *free jazz*. Coleman favoured the white Grafton acrylic alto which had also been occasionally used by Parker (for instance, in his celebrated 1953 concert at Massey Hall, Toronto) and in England, briefly, by John Dankworth.

Apollo   New York's Apollo Theatre is especially significant as a venue in the formative years of orchestral jazz: *Duke* Ellington's, Fletcher Henderson's and Chick Webb's were among the bands which performed there; Webb's subsequently world-famous vocalist *Ella* Fitzgerald made an early appearance at one of the Apollo's Amateur Nights.

Arcadia   A ballroom in St Louis: Bix Beiderbecke and Pee Wee Russell played there with Frankie Trumbauer's band in 1926.

Archer Street   This small Soho street was the meeting-place for London jazz musicians in the 1930s. Godbolt describes it as 'their open-air club' (Godbolt, 183), and his fascinating pages on 'Archer Street Jazzmen' usefully document British jazz's creative cross-fertilisation with (and financial dependence upon) commercial *dance-band* music.

Armstrong, Louis See *Satchmo*.

Austin High Though schools seldom figure as focal points in
jazz history, *Chicago*'s Austin High is an exception: 'I suppose,'
said Jimmy McPartland, 'everyone who has read about the jazz
of the twenties knows the name Austin High School Gang'
(quoted in Shapiro, 122). McPartland himself was among its
members; so were Frank Teschemacher and Bud Freeman; and
young Benny Goodman 'came out there and sat in with the
Austin gang' (Shapiro, 128). Of course, it can be argued that
this was a kind of secondary imitative jazz, evolved by an enthu-
siastic bunch of white musicians who happened to meet at
school; but in this respect Austin High set an example which
was to be followed in other schools throughout the world,
though usually with less distinguished results.

Baddest   According to Jonathon Green, '(US Black use) the very best, supreme' (Green, 10): it sounds like a young, fairly recent usage, but Billy Taylor, recalling pre-war jazz musicians in Washington D.C., described Harold Francis and Toby Walker as 'the baddest piano players in town. Everybody aspired to do what they did...' (quoted in Gitler, 108). 'Trumpet players love to play with great drummers,' said Miles Davis of Tony Williams, 'and I could definitely hear right away that this was going to be one of the baddest motherfuckers who had ever played a set of drums' (quoted in the *Independent*, 26 February 1997).

Bags   The nickname of vibraphone player Milt Jackson: see *MJQ*. The bags in question were allegedly those under his eyes after demob celebrations.

ball   In *Hear Me Talkin' to Ya*, the *New Orleans* clarinetist Alphonse Picou remembered his audition with the Excelsior Band in 1895: 'That was on a Thursday night, the rehearsal, and on the Saturday night following they had an engagement to play a ball (at that time the dances were called balls) on Liberty Street' (quoted in Shapiro, 33). The word thus used is common in jazz titles such as Shelton Brooks's 'Darktown Strutters Ball' (1915), but it also figures in its slang sense of 'a good time' or more specifically 'sexual intercourse' (Green, 12): when Carmen McRae sings, with relish, 'But I ball all day Sunday', the sleevenote demurely prints 'bawl', but that is not what she means (*Live at Sugar Hill*, Time, 1964).

ballad   In this context, 'the typical popular song adapted from ordinary commercial music' (Newton, 18). See *standard song*.

bandwagon   Early New Orleans bands either marched through the city or travelled along the streets on carts known as *band wagons* (Berendt, 11): they were at the heart of New Orleans street life, hence 'to jump on the bandwagon' means 'to join in any popular and currently successful movement in the hope of gaining advantage from it' (Chambers).

banjo   In general, 'jazz instrumentation no doubt derives from Europe; but the banjo, which took the place of the guitar in early jazz, was an invention of the Negro' (Berendt, 279). Both the limited range and the perkily comical tone of the *banjo* counted against it as jazz rapidly became more sophisticated and more orchestrally ambitious during the 1920s, though it retained a place in folk music and *skiffle*. It was naturally a much-prized ingredient in revivalist bands and in *trad* jazz, to which it usually contributed a dispiriting rhythmic sluggishness. The word is a corruption of *bandore*, an Elizabethan wire-stringed instrument. To British ears, of course, the instrument – in its more diminutive version, the ukulele – is inseperable from the personality of George Formby and thus inherently ludicrous.

bar The two most widely-used musical forms in jazz are the 12-*bar blues* and the 32-*bar standard song*: if these sound unduly simple or restrictive, they might usefully be compared to, respectively, the sonnet and the lyric poem: in other words, they are structures inviting almost limitless creative variation. Bars of another sort also figure significantly in jazz history, as will be clear from entries elsewhere in this book.

baritone Apart from the seldom-used bass saxophone (whose only notable jazz practitioner was Adrian Rollini), the *baritone* is the largest and deepest-pitched of the sax family. It is almost too characterful an instrument, with a bitter-sweetly melancholic and intimately conversational tone, as if it wants to snuggle up and confide in the listener. It was an invaluable addition to Ellington's musical palette, in the hands of the incomparable Harry Carney, and its unique voicings added colour to the reed sections of other jazz and dance bands, including Glenn Miller's. Gerry Mulligan subsequently made it an equally distinctive feature of the post-war *modern* jazz scene: see also *hip*.

barrelhouse A piano style which evolved into *boogie woogie*, from which it is not clearly distinguishable, named after small drinking-places 'serving beer from the wood, which is unusual in the USA, where most beer is bottled' (Panassié, 19) or – rather more convincingly – 'so called because the room with the piano usually had a bar consisting of a barrel of whisky resting on two planks' (Clarke, 138). Clarke also provides a likeable explanation of the predominant and repetitive left hand which is characteristic of *barrelhouse* pianists: 'They played a rolling rhythm in the left hand (eight notes to the bar) so that they could reach for a drink or a sandwich with the right hand.' Barrelhouse pianists included Cow Cow Davenport and Pinetop Smith, whose recording of 'Pinetop's Boogie Woogie' (Brunswick, 1928) is a relatively rare example of an under-documented style.

Basin Street The most famous street in the *Storyville* district of *New Orleans*, celebrated in Spencer Williams's 1923 composition 'Basin Street Blues'. The definitive recording is by Louis Armstrong (Okeh, 1928); it does not include the somewhat anachronistic verse (beginning 'Won't you come along with me / To the Mississippi …') which was 'added in 1931 by Glenn Miller and Jack Teagarden when they recorded the number under the name of the Charleston Chasers' (Panassié, 22).

bass The string *bass*'s indispensable place in jazz was established surprisingly late, in the mid-1920s: the bass-line in *New Orleans* marching-bands was of course carried by the *tuba*, and this anachronistically survived until the introduction of electric microphones, since acoustic recording horns were unable to pick up the string bass accurately (or at all); the grumbly-toned bass saxophone added colour to some early bands, but this too was seldom heard after the 1920s.

The string bass-player's role is clearly vital but essentially supporting, and bass solos are generally an unwelcome rarity. By an odd quirk of fate, two of jazz's outstanding bassists – who *could* create welcome solos – died young: Jimmy Blanton, who during two years with a vintage Ellington band 'revolutionised jazz bass playing' (*JOR* [2], 81), died of tuberculosis in 1942; while Scott La Faro, equal partner with drummer Paul Motian in a fine Bill Evans Trio, was killed in a car accident in 1961. The outstanding bass-players in modern jazz are Oscar Pettiford, an undervalued pioneer of *bebop*; Ray Brown, a long-serving member of the Oscar Peterson Trio and stalwart of numerous Norman Granz-produced sessions; and Charles Mingus, whose solo in 'Mood Indigo' (Impulse, 1963) is both a homage to *Duke* Ellington and, as Nat Hentoff writes in his sleevenote, 'an indication that … there is no bassist in jazz who combines so authoritative a command of the instrument with so resourceful and passionate an imagination.'

battle Although *New Orleans* bands could be fiercely competitive, the term *battle of the bands* is primarily associated with the ballroom circuit of the south-west, where challenges were held from the mid-1920s to the early 1940s: 'Each local band played opposite each visiting band at the town's local balllroom' (Franklin S. Driggs, in Hentoff, 194).

Beale Street W. C. Handy, who had already published his 'Memphis Blues' in 1912, celebrated this Memphis street in

'Beale Street Blues' (1916); James Baldwin entitled his 1974 novel of 'black survival and eventual triumph' *If Beale Street Could Talk*.

Bean The nickname of tenor-saxophonist Coleman Hawkins (1904–69; also known as Hawk) who, though he denied 'that he was the first man to play jazz on the tenor sax' (*JOR* [1], 163), was beyond doubt the instrument's earliest major and lastingly influential stylist. The first phase of his career was spent with Fletcher Henderson's orchestra, the one band to rival Ellington's in significance and (thanks to Don Redman's arrangements) sophistication. During the mid-1930s he spent five years in Europe, and it was on his return to America in 1939 that his second phase – leading small groups grounded in the swing era but with prescient hints of post-war modernism – began; this period includes fine recordings with the *Chocolate Dandies* (Commodore, 1940), Leonard Feather's All-Stars (Commodore, 1943), and a variety of outstanding musicians including Roy Eldridge and Teddy Wilson (Keynote, 1944). In the 1950s he re-invented himself yet again, as a player wholly capable of working with a bebop iconoclast such as Thelonious *Monk* but most at ease in the modified mainstream context of *The High and Mighty Hawk* (Felsted, 1958), with Buck Clayton and Hank Jones among others, one of the great jazz albums.

beat[1] The basic rhythmic unit of jazz and most other forms of music, as in 'four [beats] to the *bar*'; the phrase 'beat music', used as a synonym for early 1960s pop, is merely tautological.

beat[2] The 'Beat Generation' of American writers – Gregory Corso, Lawrence Ferlinghetti, Allen Ginsberg, Jack Kerouac and others – had an especially close affinity with post-war *bebop* or 'modern' jazz. 'Beat means beatitude, not beat up,' said Kerouac. 'You *feel* this. You feel it in a beat, in jazz – real cool jazz, or a good gutty rock number' (*The Beats*, ed. Park Honan, 147). As John Clellon Holmes puts it: 'In the arts, modern jazz is almost exclusively the music of the Beat Generation, as poetry (at least until Kerouac's novel) is its literature. If the members of this generation attend to a wailing sax in much the same way as men once used to attend to the words and gestures of sages, it is because jazz is primarily the music of inner freedom, of improvisation, of the creative individual rather than the interpretative group' (*The Beats*, 155). Yet this is perhaps to undervalue both the self-disciplined precision and the collaborative interaction of the jazz performance, as opposed to the perceived jazz lifestyle, an emphasis reaffirmed when Holmes proposes a parallel between 'the short, violent life of altosaxist Charlie Parker' and those of James Dean and Dylan Thomas. Nevertheless, the beat poets at their best come closer than any other group of writers to catching in print the tone and texture, at once smoky and luminous, of 'modern' jazz, as in these lines from 'Way Out West' by Le Roi Jones:

> Morning: some tear is broken
> on the wooden stairs
> of my lady's eyes. Profusions
> of green. The leaves. Their
> constant prehensions. Like old
> junkies on Sheridan square, eyes
> cold and round. There is a song
> Nat Cole sings ... This city
> & the intricate disorder
> of the seasons.
>
> (*Beat Poets*, ed. Gene Baro, 34)

bebop 'Of all the uncommunicative, secret-society terms that jazz has surrounded itself with,' says Whitney Balliett, 'few are more misleading than "bebop"' (*Dinosaurs in the Morning*, 18). The central, characteristic style of small-group modern jazz which evolved principally in *Kansas City* and New York during the early 1940s 'was named bebop, a word which mirrored, onomatopoetically, the then best-loved interval of the music: the flatted fifth' (Berendt, 18–19); Stearns, on the other hand, endorses Maurice Crane's suggestion that the word derives from 'the Spanish expression "Arriba!" or "Riba!" (literally: "up"), which is the Afro-Cuban musician's equivalent for "Go!"' (Stearns, 155). Joachim Berendt lists the 'most important musicians who gathered at Minton's' (in Harlem) as *Dizzy* Gillespie (trumpet), Charlie Parker (alto), Thelonious *Monk* (piano), Charlie Christian (guitar) and Kenny Clarke (drums): this clearly represents an unusual concentration of gifted, innovative musicians in a single place. Against this should be set Balliett's diagnosis of a 'final confusing peculiarity of bebop': 'although Parker, Gillespie, and Monk, each of whom possessed enormous talent, emerged at about the same time, they never enjoyed the spotlight simultaneously, as did such slightly older men as Hawkins, Eldridge, Art Tatum, and Sidney Catlett' (*Dinosaurs in the Morning*, 20). Leonard Feather is probably right to counsel against any attempt to locate *bebop*'s origins too precisely: 'Bebop actually was a synthesis of many musical ideas, created by a disparate group of musicians who were often unaware of the startling impact their innovations would have' (*From Satchmo to Miles*, 129).

Bebop, or rebop, or simply bop, is characterised by scurryingly virtuosic phrasing, audaciously fragmented harmonics and an astonishing degree of re-inventive fecundity which often builds on the skeletal chord-structures of old numbers: the effect, typically, is of a steady mellow light transformed into dazzling prismatic refractions. Edmund White's semi-fictional narrator recalls hanging out with art students and 'listening to the newest bop, those cool blue blips and pop-eyed blasts, muted ballads or zany callisthenics' (*The Beautiful Room is Empty*, 3). Some sternly traditional critics predictably took a dim view of this: Rex Harris thought that the 'meaningless displays of grotesque technique and mathematical chord and harmonic progressions' in bebop produced 'the same amount of pleasure as a Euclid theorem' (Harris, 172); while Panassié decided that bebop was not a form of jazz at all but 'a type of music which has wrongly been described as jazz' (Panassié, 36). But in a longer perspective things look – or sound – very different: indeed, the disciplined creative energy of a Charlie Parker Quintet of the 1940s has more in common with the Louis Armstrong Hot Five of the 1920s than with much music of the intervening *swing* era, and seems arguably to represent both a return to and a remaking of fundamental jazz principles.

belly fiddle   According to a 1939 'Vocabulary of Swing Terms', this was a term for the *guitar* (*PBJ*, 134).

big band   The typical jazz unit of the early 1920s comprised anything from a solo pianist up to a five- or seven-piece group; and this would be equally true of jazz thirty years later, in the early 1950s. The *big band*, of a dozen or more musicians, evolved during the latter part of the 1920s, assisted by a variety of factors: the successive dance crazes which typified the *jazz age*; the rise of the saxophone family as acceptable, and ultimately dominant, jazz instruments; the revolution in recording techniques which enabled richer orchestral textures to be captured on disc; and, by no means least, the influence of ambitious and gifted arrangers such as *Duke* Ellington and Don Redman. At best, the big bands extended the boundaries of jazz and greatly enriched its musical possibilities; they also heralded the arrival of the *swing* era, with its vulgar extremes, and – a little later –

the anaemic though hugely popular music of Glenn Miller. Economic conditions after World War II killed off all but the hardiest of jazz big bands, while the arrival of *rock 'n' roll* extinguished what was the left of them in pop music. Among more recent attempts to create a genuine jazz big band, a notable one is the multi-national Kenny Clarke-Francy Boland Big Band, to be heard in spectacular form on the album *Doing Time* (Black Lion, 1971).

Bird The alto-saxophonist Charlie Parker (1920–55), universally known as *Bird* or *Yardbird*, was the defining musician of *bebop* and one of the half-dozen most influential figures in the history of jazz; his characteristic self-introduction, as Bob Reisner recalled, was: 'I'm Charlie Parker. People call me Bird' (*Bird: The Legend of Charlie Parker*, 13). According to Jay McShann, the name derived from an incident which took place on the way to a *gig*: some chickens ran across the road and one was run over; Parker insisted on stopping to retrieve it. When they reached their digs, Parker explained to their landlady: 'Miss, we ran over the yardbird on our way here, just a little ways out of here, and he's still warm, and I wonder if you could cook him for me?' She did. 'And from then on we started calling him "Yardbird"' (quoted in Gitler, 66).

Unlike musicians of comparable importance, such as Louis Armstrong or *Duke* Ellington, who enjoyed long and prolific careers, Parker produced his significant recorded work in one hectic decade. Apart from miscellaneous recordings, usually for minor labels, and *air-shots*, it consists of three main segments. Firstly, the sessions for *Savoy*[2]: four sides with the Tiny Grimes Quintet in September 1944 ('Tiny's Tempo', matrix S5710, has some claim to be the earliest indispensable bebop track); five in November 1945 which brought Bird and Miles Davis together on record for the first time; then a series of recordings in 1947-8, with Davis, Bud Powell, Duke Jordan or John Lewis (piano), Tommy Potter or Curley Russell (bass) and Max Roach (drums). Secondly, the recordings for *Dial*, including the notorious 'Lover Man' session of July 1946 and, much more usefully, his post-breakdown return to the studio in February 1947 (the 'Cool Blues' set with Erroll Garner) and the quintet tracks of October-November 1947 (with Davis, Jordan, Potter and Roach) – among them a marvellously re-invented 'Embraceable You'. Thirdly, the work produced by Norman Granz from 1948 onwards for Clef/Norgran/*Verve*: Granz typically teamed Parker with 'Machito and his Afro-Cubans', with a Hollywoodsized string orchestra, and with a variety of jazz 'all-star' groups, not all of them ideally compatible with Bird; at best, as in the momentous 'Funky Blues' session of June 1952 (with Johnny Hodges, Ben Webster and Oscar Peterson among the performers), the results could be magnificent.

Philip Larkin famously thought that Bird had more or less finished off jazz: 'Parker himself,' he wrote, 'compulsively fast and showy, couldn't play four bars without resorting to a peculiarly irritating five-note cliché ... his tone, though much better than that of some of his successors, was thin and sometimes shrill' (Larkin, 8). And Larkin was half-right: Parker's tone could certainly be unusually hard-edged, even abrasive, and this wasn't at all what pre-bebop-conditioned ears expected from a saxophonist – even though they might admire it in a trumpeter. Parker redefined the dynamics of the jazz quintet: one might say that he treated the alto as if it were a trumpet, just as Miles Davis treated the trumpet as if it were an alto. As for the showiness and the five-note cliché, the music must speak for itself: Bird no longer sounds (to these ears, at least) at all pointlessly flamboyant, and that five-note signature is no more intrusive than similar gestures in, say, Armstrong. Larkin grumpily noted that by 1961 'Parker was dead and a historical figure, in young eyes probably indistinguishable from King Oliver and other founding figures' (Larkin, 9): he meant that to be a joke, of course, but it seems about right. Incidentally, away from that deliberately coat-trailing Introduction to *All What Jazz*, even Larkin could be shrewdly appreciative of Parker, for instance describing him as 'a man who not only could translate his ideas into notes at superhuman speed, but who was simultaneously aware of half a dozen ways of resolving any musical situation, and could somehow refer to all of them in passing beyond it' (Larkin, 30).

When Parker died in 1955, one graffiti-inscription spread with eerie spontaneity throughout America: 'Bird Lives!'

Birdland Established in 1950 and named in homage to Charlie Parker, *Birdland* in New York is the world's most famous modern jazz club; even those who are unaware of the venue will probably have heard the theme-song composed for it by George Shearing in 1952, 'Lullaby of Birdland'.

Bird of Paradise One of a flight of ornithological titles associated with Charlie Parker, 'Bird of Paradise' (Dial, 1947) perfectly exemplifies a common *bebop* practice: it is, as Alun

Morgan explained in his sleevenote to the album *Bird Symbols* (Verve, 1962), 'the third complete master of "All the Things You Are"; on the "A" take Parker played Kern's melody in the first sixteen bars but by the time the third take was completed only the chord structure of the original remained'. Jerome Kern's tune, with its infamously wayward modulations, was a favourite starting-point for adventurous bop musicians; but the process lucidly described by Morgan had an additional attraction for cash-strapped jazz record producers who could class tracks like 'Bird of Paradise' as Parker originals, thus saving the expense of royalty payments to Kern's publishers.

Birks   The unpromising middle name of John Birks Gillespie is immortalised in the title 'Birks' Works'; see *Dizzy*.

biscuit   Gregory R. Staats notes that in blues lyrics 'A desirable young girl is likely to be called a "biscuit", while a good lover is a "biscuit roller"' (*PBJ*, 90).

Bix   Trumpeter Leon 'Bix' Beiderbecke 'is – more than any other musician – the essence of Chicago style' (Berendt, 44). Beiderbecke died in 1931, at the age of 28, and it has been intriguingly suggested that had he lived longer 'he would have ended up happily and successfully playing alongside Charlie Parker' (*JOR* [1], 42); as it is, he is best known for his recordings with Frankie Trumbauer's Orchestra, such as 'Singin' the Blues' (Okeh, 1927).

Black Bottom   'Black Bottom Stomp' is 'a beautiful example of [Jelly Roll] Morton's talent for composition' (Mick Hamer, *Listener*, 26 March 1981), whereas 'The Black Bottom' (credited to de Sylva, Brown and Henderson) is a popular song of the mid-1920s; see *Charleston*.

Black and Tan Fantasy   This 1926 composition by *Duke* Ellington and Bubber Miley proved beyond reasonable doubt that jazz could embrace structural sophistication and classical allusion – the piece ends with that famous funereal quotation from Chopin – without compromising its authenticity. The promiscuously-recording Ellington orchestra made three versions, all of them wonderful, between April and November 1927 for Brunswick, Victor and *Okeh*; it became a permanent fixture in the band's repertoire – there is a dramatic performance, for instance, in a 1955 session for Capitol. Ellington, in a moment of grandiloquent irony quoted in a sleevenote to *The Ellington Era* (Columbia, 1963), recalled that 'the Black and Tan was a speakeasy of the period where people of all races and colours mixed together for the purpose of fulfilling their social aspirations'.

Blackhawk The best-known jazz club in Los Angeles, a focal point for the *West Coast* musicians of the 1950s.

blackstick A largely obsolete slang term, like *liquorice stick*, for the *clarinet*.

Black Swan Harry Pace's New York-based Black Swan, founded in 1921 and sold to Paramount in 1924, was the first black-owned record label; Fletcher Henderson worked for it, providing arrangements and accompaniments for blues singers such as Alberta Hunter. Its motto was: 'The only genuine coloured record. Others are only passing for coloured' (quoted in Hentoff, 179).

Blind Lemon The 'best-known rural blues singer of the 1920s' (Tirro, 125), Blind Lemon Jefferson (1897–1931) occupies a position parallel to that of *Ma* Rainey; he too had a short but prolific recording career – between 1925 and 1930 – and 'he completely transcended the limitations of regional style, creating melodic patterns which were to influence singers in rural and urban areas' (*JOR* [1], 188).

blow Just as *horn* can be applied indiscriminately to instruments other than brass and woodwinds, so *blow* is a 'verb used to describe the playing of any jazz instrument, whether actually blown or not' (Ulanov, 96).

blowing session A *blowing session* involves a group of musicians playing in a particularly informal, uninhibited way: 'The countless "blowing sessions" recorded by East Coast jazz labels in the 1950s and early 1960s took the place of the jam sessions and cutting contests of earlier times' (Clarke, 348); a 'key figure in the proliferation of the spontaneous sounding "blowing session" album was a no-nonsense recording engineer, Rudy Van Gelder' (Priestley, 109).

blue In its adjectival sense of 'pensively melancholic', *blue* is not precisely the same as *blues*: if it were, the Armstrong Hot

Seven title 'Melancholy Blues' would be absurdly tautological.
Seeking earlier examples of this sense, Tirro finds David Garrick
'troubled wth ye Blews' in 1741 and Washington Irving
describing a friend in 1807 as 'under the influence of a whole
legion of the blues' (Tirro, 114). Clearly, colours are often associated with specific human characteristics – for instance, yellow
with cowardice, green with envy, and blue with unhappiness (of
a sometimes self-indulgent and even not wholly unpleasant
kind). The adjective turns up in titles such as 'Blue Moon', 'Blue
Room', 'Blue Sands', 'Blue Tune' and – with a very different
connotation – 'Blue Skies'; or alternatively, to designate a particular musician's reworking of the blues, in pieces like 'Blue
Lester' and 'Blue Monk'. The most intensely pensive melan-
cholia of all, of course, needs a shade beyond blue – and finds
it in Ellington's 'Mood Indigo'.

blue note[1]   The flattened seventh – e.g. B♭ in the key of C, E♭
in the key of F – which supplies jazz's characteristic tone of unre-
solved plangency and which, in its harmonic 'impurity',
scandalised early classically-trained critics.

Blue Note[2]   A New York label founded in 1939 by Alfred Lion
and Frank Wolff, which produced many pioneering modern jazz
recordings (including work by Bud Powell, Thelonious *Monk*,
Miles Davis and John Coltrane), before settling into a rather
more predictable house-style based on such performers as Art
Blakey, Freddie Hubbard and Horace Silver.

blues   One of the commonest misapprehensions in music is the
notion that the *blues* is a sort of Mk.I. version from which jazz
evolved, whereas it is much more interestingly just one formative and continuing strand in a complex musical genre (the same
mistake is sometimes made about *ragtime*). The blues is jazz's
most purely Afro-American component, contributing both the
formal and harmonic qualities – the 12-bar unit and the ubiquitous flattened seventh – which most obviously distinguish it
from European music. W. C. Handy said: 'The blues came from
the man farthest down. The blues came from nothingness, from
want, from desire. And when a man sang or played the blues, a
small part of the want was satisfied from the music' (quoted in
Shapiro, 258).
    Frank Tirro proposes a sensible tripartite division: the *country
blues*, 'a rural folk expression usually performed by a male
singer'; the *classic blues*, 'often sung by women, [which] bridged

the gap between folk music and the entertainment world'; and the *city blues*, which 'gave voice to the more callous aspects of ghetto life and attitudes' (Tirro, 118). It is worth noting that the blues is the one ingredient in early jazz which was primarily *sung*; almost all subsequent jazz singing derives from the blurring of repertoire with dance music which took place in the late 1920s and which introduced vocal breaks into jazz versions of *standard songs*.

'At its simplest,' says Marshall Stearns, 'the harmony of the blues consists of the three basic chords in our musical language' (Stearns, 77): that is, tonic, sub-dominant and dominant. Stearns points out that the same chords occur in, for instance, 'Yankee Doodle', 'Silent Night' and 'Swanee River': they are by no means specific to the blues, but it is the perfect simplicity of the underlying structure which permits an infinite variety of interpretation. First, of course, the jazz musician will colour those chords with sevenths and diminished sevenths (i.e. flattening everything but the tonic – a useful transitional trick). A favourite device was the 'Dixieland Change', in which the movement from C in bar 8 to G7 in bar 10 was accomplished via B7, B♭7, A7, D7 and thus to G7. But a sophisticated performer could go much further than that. Here, for instance, are twelve random bars of Art Tatum, transposed to C by Brian Townend:

C7 - - - | E7 - - - | Am - - G♯° | Gm7 - C9 - |
F7 - C7 E7 | F7 - F♯° - | C7 C♯° G7 D♯ | C G♭m7 E♭m7 A♭m7 |
Dm11 - G13 C♯° - | Dm7♭5 - C G7 | C - F7 Dm7♭5 | C - Gaug5 - |

The process of enrichment is clear, the harmonic density becoming still more intense in the blues interpretations of musicians such as Charlie Parker.

bomb   A punctuating, off-beat bass-drum effect, much employed in *bebop* and after, and not universally liked: Balliett complains of 'the relentless use of bass-drum explosions or "bombs"' (*Dinosaurs in the Morning*, 26). In the 1940s Kenny Clarke 'became famous for "dropping bombs" ... later explaining (not altogether convincingly) that his foot got tired' (Clarke, 264).

bone   An occasionally-used abbreviation of *trombone*.

boogie woogie   'A primitive manner of playing the blues on piano' is how Hugues Panassié, usually so favourably disposed

towards the earlier forms of jazz, describes *boogie woogie*
(Panassié, 35). That other arch-traditionalist Rex Harris is
friendlier though mildly apologetic: for him, it is 'a school of
piano playing which developed from the guitar style of
wandering musicians in the Southern States, and which has been
given the unfortunately puerile label of "Boogie-Woogie"'
(Harris, 140). John Steiner points out that although boogie
woogie tended to develop into 'a velocity exercise or muscular
display', originally 'it had been more beautifully a blues song
with a kind of rocking accompaniment' (Hentoff, 143). The
drawback of boogie woogie, apart from its name, lies in the
repeated figuration of the left-hand 'walking bass', which is by
definition harmonically restrictive and rhythmically monotonous. Jimmy Yancey claimed to be the inventor of boogie
woogie, though the first recorded use of the term was by Pinetop
Smith in 1928; other notable boogie pianists included Albert
Ammons, Pete Johnson and Meade Lux Lewis; and the style
was most successfully adapted and popularised during the 1930s
by *Fats* Waller. As Hoagy Carmichael put it, in 'Mr Music
Master', 'Round about 1935, you begin to hear swing, boogie
woogie and jive' – thus neatly bracketing three ways in which
jazz was made commercially marketable. Since boogie woogie
was really a somewhat constricting form of jazz, the contemporary slang use of the term 'boogie' – 'to enjoy oneself, have a
party, a good time' (Green, 29) – seems slightly anachronistic.

bop See *bebop*.

bossa nova A fusion of Brazilian and jazz elements made world-
famous by Stan Getz and Charlie Byrd in their album *Jazz
Samba* and the hit single taken from it, 'Desafinado' (Verve,
1962).

bounce A *swing* term for 'prominent rhythm' (*PBJ*, 134),
which consequently features in titles such as 'Esquire Bounce'.

box This rather dated slang term means the *piano*: the implication is that the instrument in question is likelier to be a jangling
upright than a Steinway grand.

break Although a *break* is 'any phrase played without the accompaniment of the rhythm section' (Panassié, 38), many players
and listeners use the word to mean simply a very short solo:

thus, a pair of *front line* players swapping phrases of a bar or two are said to be 'trading breaks'.

breakdown Originally, a square dance (Stearns, 140); hence, used in the titles of numbers such as Ellington's 'Birmingham Breakdown' (Vocalion, 1926) and Morton's 'Chicago Breakdown', which was recorded by Armstrong (Okeh, 1927).

Brute 'The Brute' was Willie 'The *Lion*' Smith's reciprocal nickname for the pianist James P. Johnson.

Buddy Bolden Around 1900, Bolden was leader of the first *New Orleans* jazz band: according to Bunk Johnson, 'It was the town's talk, King Bolden's band' (Shapiro, 44). He is immortalised in anecdotes – 'When they heard his horn, people would say: "Buddy Bolden is calling his children home"' (Berendt, 33) – and in the blues 'I Thought I Heard Buddy Bolden Say', a tune famously arranged by *Jelly Roll* Morton and recorded by his New Orleans Jazzmen featuring Sidney Bechet (RCA Victor, 1939). Bolden's early life was colourful but obscure: 'Nothing much is known for certain about Bolden's career in turn-of-the-century New Orleans, although they say that he worked as a barber, that he edited a scandal sheet, and that, on a clear night, his cornet could be heard all the way across the 14-mile width of Lake Pontchartrain' (Richard Williams, *Independent on Sunday*, 7 August 1994). In 1907 he was committed to a mental hospital and, when temporarily released ten years later, had no recollection of his musical past; he died in 1931. Among the many documents about him in the hospital files, 'There is not one word … stating that Buddy Bolden was a musician: a creative musician in a branch of music chosen and in part created by him' (Berendt, 35).

Bunk William 'Bunk' Johnson (1879–1949) is a reminder of how short jazz history is, and how long: short, because this legendary cornetist, only a year younger than *Buddy Bolden* (with whom he played), lived beyond the Second World War; long, because although his life (just) overlapped with mine, neither I nor anyone else has any idea of how he sounded in his prime. After those early days, Johnson retired for forty years, 'only to be dragged out by the merciless enthusiasm of the jazz revival of the 1940s' (*JOR* [1], 190); he then began to record quite prolifically, and the titles made for American Music in 1944 are widely admired, but they are something other and odder than the historical documents for which they may be mistaken.

Burgundy Street A street in *New Orleans*, east of *Storyville* and parallel with the Mississippi, which gave its name to 'Burgundy Street Blues', an evocative and nostalgic composition by George Lewis, a key figure in the New Orleans revival of the 1940s.

C melody sax 'In the saxophone family,' says Leonard Feather, 'the C Melody is the Ishmael among Aunt Hagar's children' (*BOJ*, 106); it was essentially designed to save amateur players the bother of transposition. Frankie Trumbauer was the only musician of consequence to make it his own: he, in Laurie Wright's nicely-judged phrase, is 'to the C-Melody sax what Sidney Bechet is to the soprano' (*JOR* [2], 290) – i.e. the only person to have made even the slightest sense of the thing. Its range is similar to that of the *alto*, but it has an unusually creamy – or even glutinous – tone.

Café Society This was a nightclub in Greenwich Village which 'had paved the way, from 1938, by encouraging integration both in its clientèle and its entertainment' (*BOJ*, 46): Joe Sullivan's mixed sextet played at Café Society in 1939.

cakewalk The *cakewalk* was a syncopated dance which became fashionable, like *ragtime*, in the closing years of the nineteenth century: 'The syncopated rhythm of the cakewalk was part of every American minstrel show,' says Tirro, noting also that by 1900 'contests for cakewalking and ragtime piano playing were the rage' (Tirro, 52). 'Cakewalkin' Babies' is a number recorded twice by Clarence Williams's Blue Five (also known as the *Red Onion* Jazz Babies), an extraordinary band which included both Louis Armstrong and Sidney Bechet (Gennett, 1924). It would be ungenerous here to omit one of the world's great crossword clues: 'A cakewalk – that's plenty (9)'. The solution is on p.151.

calliope A set of keyboard-operated steam whistles: 'One of the most beautiful sounds in the city of New Orleans was Fate Marable playing his steam calliope about seven in the evening ... to let the people know the boats were going to cut out on excursions' (Danny Baker, quoted in Shapiro, 83). There would be singing guitarists on the lower deck, too, and the popularity of these entertainments led to the engagement of jazz bands on the boats.

Canal Street New Orleans 'was split by Canal Street, with one part of the people uptown and the Creoles downtown' (Danny Baker, quoted in Shapiro, 20): it runs in a south-easterly direction from the New Orleans Navigation Canal to the Mississippi, passing through *Storyville*.

canary This was a *swing* era term for a 'girl vocalist' (*PBJ*,

134), mainly applied to the 'sweet' singers with dance bands since it hardly suits the more robust vocalists of jazz.

Carnegie Hall The first jazz concert to be held in New York's Carnegie Hall featured Benny Goodman: 'If there is one outstanding example of the Goodman band at its peak it is the [Columbia] recordings from the famous 1938 Carnegie Hall Concert' (*JOR* [2], 113); the second, a few months later, was John Hammond's almost equally celebrated *Spirituals to Swing* compendium. The Goodman concert, on 16 January 1938, was certainly a milestone in jazz history: 'That night at Carnegie,' he recalled later, 'was a great experience, because it represented something – a group of musicians going on stage and playing tunes by Gershwin and Berlin and Kern in arrangements by Fletcher [Henderson] and Edgar Sampson, getting up and playing the choruses the way they wanted to, each of them just being himself – and holding the attention of all those people for two hours and a half' (Shapiro, 312). As the auditorium filled up, Harry James reportedly said, 'I feel like a waitress on a date with a college boy,' or, according to Bobby Hackett and perhaps more convincingly, 'I feel like a whore in church' (quoted by Larkin, 21).

Something like jazz had, however, been heard at Carnegie Hall very much earlier, as Frank Tirro points out: in May 1912, Jim Europe, 'the most influential black musician in New York', directed an orchestra who 'played and sang in syncopated style, and although professional criticism was mixed, they seem to have had a dynamic impact upon their audience' (Tirro, 58).

Carolina Shout An immensely influential composition by James P. Johnson, who recorded it on a piano roll from which both *Duke* Ellington and *Fats* Waller learned the fingering; Johnson's earliest (acoustic) gramophone recording of it was made for Okeh in 1924, and he re-recorded it for Decca in 1944.

Casa Loma Named after a Canadian night-club, the Casa Loma Orchestra was one of the earliest *swing* bands whose 'somewhat unique contribution to jazz took place in 1931, for the band acquired a trumpet screamer, Sonny Dunham, and his sound soon became a standard part of the American big-band vocabulary' (Tirro, 226); they succeeded the Claude Hopkins band in a residency at *Roseland* in 1934.

cat[1] Jonathon Green suggests: 'from jazz use, c. 1950s poss. fr.

"alligator", early black use for worldly, smart, sophisticated male' (Green, 46): the 'alligator' derivation (alligator = gator = gate = cat) looks pretty tenuous to me, while the obvious synonym for 'worldly, smart, sophisticated' is of course *cool* – hence 'cool cat'. Barry Ulanov proposes a different etymology: he suggests that because much early jazz 'was bordello or *cathouse* music, its performers were called *cats*, and by many still are' (Ulanov, 89). The word has long been a term of affectionate admiration among jazz musicians – 'You had to listen to this cat, boy,' says Howard McGhee of Louis Armstrong (quoted in Gitler, 33) – and anyone well-informed about jazz may by extension be called a cat: cf. *aficionado*.

Cat[2]   The nickname of trumpeter William 'Cat' Anderson (b.1916), probably thanks to the astonishingly dextrous high-note agility which became famous during his two lengthy spells with the Ellington band.

changes   Jazz musicians refer to a number's chord sequence, for obvious reasons, as its *changes*. In the simplest possible *blues*, these changes will involve only the three most basic chords and their related sevenths, but the music's harmonic density increased enormously during the 1920s, and with the evolution of *bebop* twenty years later the changes became both complex and, often, extremely rapid. Charlie Parker was the incomparable master of this: 'A lot of guys forget their changes,' said Shorty Baker. 'Bird would ramble, but he always got back to the key' (quoted in *Bird: The Legend of Charlie Parker*, 29).

Charleston   The tune which put Charleston, South Carolina, 'on the map' (according to its lyric) was actually composed by James P. Johnson in New York, where early in the century 'the population of the San Juan Hill area was boosted by an influx of migrants from the South, some from Alabama, some from the part of South Carolina and Georgia that centred around Charleston'; the latter, 'known as Gullahs or Geechies, had a powerful effect on the style of the local piano men' (Lyttelton, 32). According to Willie 'The *Lion*' Smith, 'the Gullahs would start out early in the evening dancing two-steps, waltzes, schottisches; but as the night wore on and the liquor began to work, they would start improvising their own steps ... it was from these improvised steps that the Charleston dance originated.' The global success of *The Charleston* – both the number itself and the dance craze triggered by it – was a very striking example of the way in which the evocative potential of Southern names could be commercially exploited (see also *Creole*); other compositions, such as 'The Black Bottom' (purportedly describing a dance which originated in the mud of the Swanee River), simultaneously parodied the Charleston and attempted to cash in on its success.

chart A band's written or printed arrangement of a particular *number*: 'You didn't say, "Let's play it like they played it." ... You said, "Hey, let's play this chart. Let's do this' (Shelley Manne, quoted in Gitler, 11); 'The up-tempo charts, for all their harmonic richness, were swung with a singular lightness' (Gitler, 252). The usage is typical of jazz musicians' habit of regarding notated music with a degree of affectionate disparagement: cf. *dots*.

Chet The hippest, coolest and most charismatically confused representative of the *beat* generation in jazz, the white *West Coast* trumpeter and vocalist Chet Baker joined the Gerry Mulligan Quartet in 1952 and was *Downbeat*'s 24-year-old New Star of 1953. Neither his inward, halting trumpet style nor his melancholic, understated singing voice (like a sort of sleep-walking Mel Tormé) in itself constitutes a major talent, but Baker was the icon jazz needed to outflank its noisy sibling, *rock 'n' roll*: 'He was James Dean, Sinatra and Bix, rolled into one' (Carr, 80). His recordings for Pacific Jazz, treated rather dismissively by some critics, have retained or regained their cult status and can still sound (to a listener in the right mood) irresistible: even his singing, once described by Alun Morgan as 'a somewhat time-consuming habit' (*JOR* [2], 12), has its distinctive charm, and the quartet session which produced 'My Funny Valentine', 'Time After Time' and 'I Fall in Love Too Easily' (Pacific Jazz, 1954) is on its own terms perfect. Drug-induced disasters – and an eventual comeback – followed his mid-1950s success; he died in 1988, after falling from a hotel window in Amsterdam.

Chicago After the closure of *Storyville*, there was a northward exodus of musicians from *New Orleans*, many of whom – including Louis Armstrong, Johnny Dodds, *Jelly Roll* Morton and King Oliver – ended up, for a while at least, in Chicago, which in consequence became 'the great centre of jazz between 1919 and 1929' (Panassié, 52): this is the traditional view and there is some truth in it, but the implied notion of jazz as a localised music which could be parcelled up and transported from New Orleans to Chicago (and thence to New York) is a ludicrous one which, as Francis Newton rightly warns, 'not only lacks much relation to the facts, but also makes it totally impossible to understand how jazz developed as it actually did' (Newton, 41). Well before 1919, New Orleans musicians had travelled widely (Morton had been to Chicago itself as early as 1907) and an already complex music had both influenced and been influenced by other styles in America and Europe. John Steiner says that in either 1910 or, probably, 1912 'both Jelly Roll Morton and Tony Jackson began playing piano and entertaining the bars of the "Section" along State Street near Thirty-fifth' (Hentoff, 141) and that around 1912 'a New Orleans clarinetist (possibly George Bacquet) sat in with [Glover Compton] at Elite No 1, causing a minor riot by his sensational display' (Hentoff, 143).

More significant than this musical peregrination was the emergence of a distinct Chicago *style*, principally developed by white musicians indebted to though not merely imitative of the arrivals from New Orleans: 'its hell-for-leather push recalled the Dixieland band and it had something of the solid beat and blues colour of Oliver' (Charles Edward Smith, in Hentoff, 37). The Chicago musicians included Eddie Condon, Bud Freeman, *Pee Wee* Russell, Muggsy Spanier and, above all, *Bix* Beiderbecke who 'is – more than any other musician – the essence of Chicago style' (Berendt, 44).

Chocolate Dandies   Between 1928 and 1940, the personnel of this celebrated *pickup* group included such eminent musicians as Benny Carter, Roy Eldridge and Coleman Hawkins.

chorus   Alongside several other meanings – such as the between-the acts commentaries in Greek drama or in Shakespeare (e.g. *Henry V*) and the band of singers in an opera, oratorio or mass – the *chorus* is commonly understood to be that part of a poem or folk song, distinct from the verse and usually repeated, which is otherwise known as the *refrain*. However, jazz and dance music record labels until the 1950s frequently bear the words 'with vocal chorus' or 'with vocal refrain' to indicate a vocal contribution of unspecified length in an otherwise instrumental performance, while 'Jazz musicians use the word "chorus" to mean a complete statement of the tune (without the introduction, typically thirty-two bars), as in "Take another chorus"'

(Clarke, 95). Though these two meanings seem to be at odds with other usage, they are perfectly clear in their contexts.

clambake   An interesting example of a word whose connotation has been almost completely reversed: 'earlier used honorifically to mean *jam session*; later used to denote an improvised or arranged session which doesn't come off' (Ulanov, 94). The Clambake Seven was a small band drawn from the Tommy Dorsey orchestra.

clarinet   For an instrument so obviously indispensable to *New Orleans* and *Dixieland* music and so firmly associated with *swing*, the *clarinet* has had a curiously chequered career in jazz. Alphonse Picou, who recalled joining Boo Boo Fortunea's band at the age of sixteen in 1895 and who went on to create the legendary solo on 'High Society', was the first of the New Orleans clarinetists. He was followed by Johnny Dodds and Sidney Bechet – yet even here the qualifications start, for Dodds is best-remembered not as a leader but as a member of the Armstrong Hot Five and Seven, while Bechet moved on to the *soprano* saxophone. Among other New Orleans-born clarinetists were Jimmy Noone, Albert Nicholas, Omer Simeon and Barney Bigard – the latter an important transitional figure who in 1928 joined the *Duke* Ellington orchestra – while the white *Chicago* school included Mezz Mezzrow, Pee Wee Russell and Frank Teschemacher. By the mid-1930s the clarinet had given jazz many fine musicians but somehow none who was unquestionably an international star on the instrument: that was to change, not quite unambiguously for the better, when Benny Goodman formed his immensely popular orchestra in 1935.

   'The clarinetist of whom the layman thinks first when the jazz clarinet is mentioned,' says Joachim Berendt, 'is Benny Goodman' (Berendt, 147). This is undoubtedly true, and nothing can detract from Goodman's success, his immense technical gifts, or the quality of the recordings he made with the band (and more especially with a small group consisting of himself, Teddy Wilson, Lionel Hampton and Gene Krupa) for RCA Victor and Columbia. Nevertheless, an element of reservation almost invariably creeps into discussions of Goodman's clarinet-playing: there is a 'lack of relaxation' and a 'detachment not compensated for by any outstanding display of formal inventiveness' (*JOR* [1], 145), an absence of 'harmonic subtlety and rhythmic complexity' (Berendt, 148); to me, Goodman usually sounds as if he's playing behind glass. This metamorphosis of a sturdy New Orleans instrument into the rather chilly embodiment of swing, coinciding with the unchallengable ascent of the *alto* and *tenor* saxophones as the predominant reed instruments, may help to explain the clarinet's decline from favour in post-war jazz. Meeting a particularly morose amateur musician during his trip down the Mississippi, Jonathan Raban notes that 'he played clarinet, the saddest instrument' (*Old Glory*, 213).

clinker A 'bad note, or one that is fluffed' (Ulanov, 94): a hazard, of course, in live performances of all kinds of music, and on records one of the reasons why one *take* may be preferred over another.

cocktail The style of piano-playing – both needlessly flashy and tediously unoriginal – which became popular in up-market bars and restaurants became derisively known as *cocktail piano*. Red Norvo remembered 'reading reviews about Art Tatum in the '30s and somebody criticized him for having too much technique – a showoff – cocktail piano, you know?' (quoted by Gitler, 49). Needless to say, Tatum is absolutely *not* a cocktail pianist, and neither is Dave Brubeck, despite Peter Russell's description of his quartet as 'purveyors of intellectualised cocktail music' (*Jazz Monthly*, June 1961, 29).

combo A *swing* era term for the combination of players in a small jazz band.

Commodore Jazz record label founded in 1938 as an offshoot of the Commodore Music Shop, New York: for it, Milt Gabler produced some of the finest small-group sessions of the *swing* era, featuring performers such as Chu Berry, Eddie Condon, Roy Eldridge and Coleman Hawkins. Commodore also released two celebrated sets of recordings made by Billie Holiday, although the most famous of these – 'Strange Fruit' (1939) – was originally intended for issue by Columbia, who found its vivid images of lynching too powerfully explosive for their own catalogue.

comp According to Panassié: 'Abbreviation for accompaniment. Applied to a piano accompaniment in regular 4/4 time ...' (Panassié, 60). But not only to the piano: 'Lend an ear to [the guitarist, Barney] Kessel, by the way, who comps sensitively behind the pianist [Oscar Peterson]' (Keith Shadwick, *Gramophone*, June 1996, 121).

Connie's Inn   A Harlem club owned by Connie and George Immerman: the Fats Waller/Andy Razaf show *Load of Coal*, which introduced the song 'Honeysuckle Rose', was staged there in 1928; *Hot Chocolates*, the following year, contained even more Waller/Razaf numbers, including 'Ain't Misbehavin'' which received its definitive performance when Louis Armstrong joined the company.

cool   A cerebral, introspective, restrained post-war style, the polar opposite of *hot* or *New Orleans* jazz. In 1948, the trumpeter Miles Davis briefly led a progressive nine-piece band which was re-formed (with some changes of personnel) to record for Capitol in 1949 and 1950: eight resulting tracks, by the 'Miles Davis Orchestra', were first issued as 78s, then as a 10-inch LP, and in 1957, with the addition of previously omitted items, as the 12-inch LP *Birth of the Cool*. Though this may be plausibly regarded as one of modern jazz's twin foundation-stones – the *bebop* recordings of Charlie Parker, with whom Davis had previously worked, forming the other – it was not until the mid 1950s that Davis's reputation became assured, with the formation of a quintet including John Coltrane: *Milestones* (Columbia, 1958) and *Kind of Blue* (Columbia, 1959), the latter featuring Cannonball Adderley and Bill Evans, represent Davis's *cool jazz* at its incomparable maturity; '*Kind of Blue* has been a cornerstone of postwar jazz for so long that it seems inconceivable any jazz fan doesn't own it' (John Fordham, *Guardian*, 17 September 1993). Other musicians of the period whose work was substantially influenced by the concept of 'cool' include *Chet* Baker, Bob Brookmeyer, Stan Getz, Gerry Mulligan and Art Pepper. See also *hip, West Coast*.

coon song   Frank Tirro defines the *coon song* as a type 'popular in the 1880s, in syncopated ragtime style, often with the lyrics that reflected the white American stereotypes of black Americans' (Tirro, 432). As implied elsewhere – see the entry under *Old Folks at Home* – this obsessive need for whites to render their perception of blacks harmless and palatable was matched by the readiness of some black musicians to embrace the same stereotypes (which thus found their way into jazz lyrics). For instance, it was the black songwriter Ernest Hogan who in 1896 published the immensely successful coon song 'All Coons Look Alike to Me', subtitled 'A Darkey Misunderstanding', which puts self-evidently white racist sentiments into the mouth of a black singer: the sheet music, complete with its extraordinary cover, is reproduced in Tirro, 63–6. In 1905, E. M. Forster used the phrase 'coon song' essentially to indicate Gino Carella's lack of decorum: 'A coon song lay open on the piano, and of the two tables one supported Baedeker's *Central Italy*, the other Harriet's inlaid box' (*Where Angels Fear to Tread*, 109). The word 'coon', an abbreviation of 'racoon', continued to be employed by some cheerfully insensitive whites until the mid-twentieth century and still persists as a term of racist abuse.

cornball   *Cornball* as noun or adjective – and in the more common adjectival form *corny* – refers to anything that it hackneyed, obvious, trite: 'The "cornball" ending lacked only the cymbal sound of a typical Guy Lombardo Mickey ending' (Tirro, 188).

cornet   Buddy Bolden, *King* Oliver, and the young Louis Armstrong all played the *cornet*; but, with rare exceptions, the instrument was replaced in jazz from the mid-1920s onwards by the *trumpet*.

Cotton Club   This New York venue of the 1920s was noted for its 'African Jungle' and immortalised by *Duke* Ellington and his Cotton Club Orchestra; 'The Cotton Club was a class house' (Louis Metcalf, quoted in Shapiro, 231), 'Harlem's most expensive night spot' (Berendt, 50). When Ellington's residency there ended in 1931, he was succeeded by Cab Calloway, 'the satin zoot-suited father of modern black dance music' (*Independent*, 20 November 1994).

Cotton Pickers   After leaving Fletcher Henderson, the great arranger Don Redman in 1928 'became musical director of MacKinney's Cotton Pickers, and made it into the finest midwestern orchestra of its day' (*JOR* [1], 264). The Cotton Pickers had been an efficient but relatively undistinguished black band from Detroit; however, 'In Redman's hands McKinney's became very much an arranger's band, the equivalent of the Miles Davis 1948 nonet' (*JOR* [2], 239), a transition of great significance on the verge of the *swing* era. Their greatest success (and theme tune), 'If I Could Be with You' (Victor, 1930), featured an alto solo by Benny Carter.

Count   William 'Count' Basie (1904–84) was an influential bandleader and a sparingly swinging pianist. During the 1930s and 1940s his orchestra included Buck Clayton, Vic Dickenson, Harry Edison, Billie Holiday and Lester Young as well as an outstanding rhythm section; after a lean time in the early 1950s, his re-formed big band was often heard accompanying star soloists such as *Ella* Fitzgerald (Verve, 1956) and Frank Sinatra (Reprise, 1962). The nickname 'Count', 'given to him by a radio announcer who thought he deserved to rank with Duke Ellington and Earl Hines' (Hardy, 43), is in a sense unhelpful, inviting direct comparison with the incomparable *Duke*. Basie was a different kind of musician altogether, an inspired facilitator rather than an original composer, who proved beyond doubt that it was possible for a big band in the *swing* era to play uncompromising jazz and whose later work for many listeners exactly defines the phrase 'big band jazz'. The affectionate regard in which he was held by his fellow-musicians is nicely conveyed by Billie Holiday's modified lyric in a 1937 broadcast performance with the Basie band of 'I Can't Get Started': 'I've been consulted by Franklin D. / Even Basie had me to tea ...'

Crane River The Crane River Jazz Band, led by Ken Colyer, was one of the pioneering post-war revivalist bands in Britain. According to George Melly, 'The Crane River is a muddy little stream which trickles past London airport on the road to Staines' (*Owning-Up*, 46): not quite the Mississippi. That sort of gentle self-deprecation has often been one of the more engaging characteristics of the British jazz scene.

Creole The '*gens de couleur* or Creoles' were members of 'the peculiar class of freed slaves which grew up in New Orleans' (Newton, 31); 'the coloured aristocracy of New Orleans' (Harris, 49). As Newton points out, early *New Orleans* jazz was much influenced by the French musical tradition, from which it derived its adapted forms of marches and dances as well as its military band instrumentation of brass and woodwinds. Jazz's rapid development in terms of sophistication and complexity owes a good deal to this source of musical literacy: 'The Creole-trained musician usually learned to read music before he learned to play by ear' (Charles Edward Smith, in Hentoff, 35). The French legacy is also evident in the dialect and the names of Creole musicians, of whom the most celebrated was undoubtedly Sidney Bechet, who was eventually to make his home in France. But, as is so often the way with the language of jazz, the word *Creole* soon acquired a much broader and less precise sense, becoming a tag employed to evoke a sultry

southern mood in song titles such as 'Creole Love Call' and
'Creole Rhapsody'. By 1958, the term had loosened to such an
alarming extent that it was possible for Elvis Presley to star in
a film called *King Creole* which was only tenuously connected
with jazz: its title song describes the eponymous hero as 'a man
in New Orleans who plays rock 'n' roll ... a guitar man with a
great big soul'.

Crescent City   A name for *New Orleans*, deriving from its
location 'on the east bank of a bend in the Mississippi in the
delta region roughly a hundred miles from its mouth' (Harris,
46).

Crowhard   In Britain during the late 1920s *Crowhard* was a
term of contempt for vociferous opponents of jazz such as Dr
Henry Coward who in 1926 described jazz, which he thought
'atavistic, lowering, degrading and a racial question', as
'composed of jingly tunes, jerky rhythms, unquestionably
grotesque forms'. Jim Godbolt adds: 'The "Crowhards"
condemned formal dance music that assaulted their ears,
thinking it to be jazz' (Godbolt, 47).

Cuban jazz   A hybrid of Afro-Cuban and jazz elements created
by Juan Tizol's composition 'Caravan', written for the *Duke
Ellington* orchestra in 1937: an interesting small-group version
of this number, featuring Tizol, was recorded by the band billed
as Duke Ellington's Coronets (Mercer, 1951). Cuba had been
significant in the pre-history of jazz as an early site of fusion
between the musics of West African slaves and of Spain: 'Cuba
gave birth to the habanera; to the rhumba, supposedly named
after a West African dance step; and to the bolero, the tango
and other forms' (*BOJ*, 12).

cutting contest   *New Orleans* bands frequently indulged in
direct musical confrontations, called *cutting contests*, and the
same principle survived in *Chicago* and *Harlem*; see also
battle.

Daddy Usually a term of affectionate respect for an elder musician (cf. *pops*), but occasionally a component of benevolent nonsense, as in Louis Armstrong's 'I'm a Ding Dong Daddy from Dumas' (Okeh, 1930).

dance bands The American and British *dance bands* of the 1930s and 1940s were conventionally viewed with amused, bemused or simply irritated contempt by jazz fans, and it is easy to see why: they traded improvised spontaneity for arranged predictability; they were largely or exclusively made up of white musicians; and their bland, characterless music proved insufferably popular while authentic jazz musicians were (as usual) enduring lean times. All this is true enough; yet jazz had always overlapped with popular dance music, and in retrospect it seems perfectly natural that the development of jazz towards more arranged forms during the *swing* era should have found its counterpart in the music of popular bands such as those led by Tommy Dorsey and Glenn Miller. Dance bands – and, increasingly, studio orchestras employing *session musicians* for film and record work – also brought some positive benefits to jazz, providing welcome employment for performers and increasing musical literacy.

In Britain, where it was necessarily an imitative art, jazz's relationship with dance music was much closer: pre-war bands such as those of Roy Fox and Lew Stone included some fluent and inventive jazz musicians; the wartime RAF band, The Squadronaires, featured the trombonist George Chisholm, one of the most gifted (and underrated) of all British jazz performers; while the enormously successful post-war big band of Ted Heath numbered among its members Kenny Baker, Don Rendell and Stan Tracey. The relationship between jazz soloist and danceband employer could, of course, have its awkward moments: Jim Godbolt recounts the story of bandleader Jack Jackson's perplexed displeasure on noticing that the dancers at Churchill's ('a plush dining and dancing establishment in New Bond Street, W1') had stopped in their tracks; the music had become 'aggressive bebop with drummer Laurie Morgan "dropping bombs" in characteristically explosive fashion and Ronnie Scott on his eighth or ninth steaming chorus' (Godbolt, 224). According to legend – and Godbolt – the ensuing dialogue between Jackson and guitarist Pete Chilver was approximately as follows. Jackson: 'What the hell's going on?' Chilver: 'Shhh, Ronnie's got the message!' Jackson: 'Give him one from me. Tell him he's got the bloody sack!'

date For the jazz musicians, a *date* is the same as an engagement or a *gig*, but Earl Hines in 'A Monday Date', recorded by Louis Armstrong and his Hot Five (Okeh, 1928), had something more intimate in mind.

Delmonico's A New York venue of the early 1930s, 'at Fifty-first Street and Broadway, underneath the old Roseland Ballroom ... Everybody used to go to Delmonico's to see Joe Venuti – there was always something going on with Joe' (Max Kaminsky, *My Life in Jazz*, 67, 69). Delmonico's was later known as *Uptown Lowdown*.

delta Invariably, the Mississippi Delta: see *Mississippi; New Orleans*.

derby A large *mute*, resembling a bowler – or in the United States a *derby* – hat: 'Marsalis flourishing one of those big-headed derby mutes usually manipulated in unison by trumpet sections' (Ronald Atkins, *Guardian*, 21 August 1993, 24).

Dial A label founded in 1946 by Ross Russell, owner of the Tempo Music Shop in Hollywood, principally to record Charlie Parker: among its most significant legacies are a Los Angeles septet session of March 1946 and two wonderful quintet sets made at New York's WOR studios in October–November 1947. These dates span Parker's 1946 breakdown, and it is unfortunate that Dial and Russell are mostly remembered for releasing the infamous 'Lover Man' recorded on the brink of it.

dig To appreciate or to understand: 'You dig?' means 'You know what I'm talking about?'

Dippermouth Blues The recording of this number by King Oliver and his Creole Jazz Band (Okeh, 1923) contains solos by Oliver (cornet) and Johnny Dodds (clarinet) and, in the final chorus, the most famous shouted exclamation in jazz: 'Oh play that thing!' The title, according to Brian Rust, refers to the fact that Oliver 'would not allow refreshments on the stand other than a bucket of sugared water with a dipper', but it is surely an alternative nickname for the number's joint composer, Louis Armstrong, otherwise known as 'satchel-mouth' or *Satchmo*.

dirty   Cited by Newton as a late-1920s synonym for *hot* (Newton, 21).

Dixieland   A combination of historical misfortune and (it must be admitted) critical prejudice against white jazz musicians has made *Dixieland* virtually synomous with second-rate imitation; and indeed it is easy enough to list those essential jazz qualities which Dixieland often seems to lack: depth, commitment, underlying seriousness. Dixieland is 'the more commercial style' (Berendt, 12) of white *New Orleans* jazz; or, more damningly, it is 'jazz which is played in a quasi-New-Orleans style by white musicians' (Harris, 65). These reservations somewhat qualify the significance of what most listeners regard as the earliest jazz records – including the Original Dixieland Jazz Band's 'Dixieland Jass Band One-Step', 'Livery Stable Blues' and 'Clarinet Marmalade' (Victor, 1917), 'Darktown Strutters' Ball' and 'Indiana' (Columbia, 1917) and 'Tiger Rag' (Aeolian, 1917). Subsequently, the term was adopted by white revivalist musicians: Muggsy Spanier, for instance, was leading a 'Dixieland Band' in the early 1950s.

Dizzy   The nickname of one of the great jazz trumpeters, John Birks Gillespie. Born in 1917, three years before Charlie Parker (with whom he is inescapably linked and compared), Gillespie possessed a highly useful combination of apparently contra-dictory talents: a leading musical innovator of the *bebop* movement, he was also an astute businessman and something of a showman in the tradition of that other great trumpeter Louis Armstrong. 'Dizzy was the smiling bopper,' wrote Dave Gelly in an obituary, yet at the same time: 'It is impossible to over-estimate the influence of John Birks Gillespie on the course of jazz, particularly on trumpet playing' (*Observer*, 10 January 1993). The bands he assembled in the 1940s, and which recorded for Musicraft (1945–6) and RCA Victor (1946–9), comprise a who's who of the post-war modern jazz movement: Dexter Gordon, Al Haig, Milt Jackson, Charlie Parker, Sonny Stitt were among their members. Gillespie and Parker were reunited on various occasions, notably the 'Quintet of the Year' concert at Massey Hall, Toronto, one of the most famous live recordings in jazz (Debut, 1953). In 1956, Gillespie became something of a cultural ambassador, leading a State Department-sponsored big band on a world tour. By this time he had joined the Norman Granz/Clef/Verve stable; Granz typically recorded him in a variety of settings, including some delightfully supple small groups – the sessions with Junior Mance, Les Spann, Sam Jones and Lex Humphries (Verve, 1959) are particularly fine.

Django One of the relatively small number of European musicians to achieve both the status of a 'jazz legend' and a popular reputation beyond jazz, Django Reinhardt was born in Belgium, of a nomadic gypsy family, in 1910. Despite receiving serious injuries in a caravan fire – which left him with two paralysed fingers – he became a highly accomplished guitarist with, necessarily, a unique and distinctive technique. The first edition of *Jazz on Record* described him as 'an exotic, a hybrid, a gypsy guitarist who brought to jazz the technique of the Pyrenees', adding that the 'result was usually stimulating, imaginative music, but rarely jazz in the normal sense of that ambiguous word' (*JOR* [1], 265). The problem implied here is compounded by the unlikely instrumentation – violin, three guitars, bass – of the Quintet of the Hot Club of France in its best-known recordings (Decca, 1938–46): an attractive, utterly unmistakable sound but one notably short of textural variety and rhythmic energy. A blistering version of 'Night and Day', recorded in Paris with some visitors from the Ellington band (Barclay, 1947), shows what Reinhardt could do when more excitingly challenged. John Lewis's composition for the Modern Jazz Quartet, 'Django' (Prestige, 1954), is a hauntingly memorable tribute to the guitarist, though without any very obvious resemblances to his style.

doo-wap A self-explanatory term derived from wordless syllables common in black pop music of the 1950s: the 'most successful doo-wap group of the fifties' (Hardy, 631) were The Platters, who exactly bridged the gap between earlier black vocal groups, such as The Ink Spots and The Mills Brothers, and the *Motown* artists of the 1960s. Like their predecessors, The Platters brought elements of jazz practice to pop music in their sentimental reworking of earlier *standard songs* such as 'Smoke Gets in Your Eyes' (Mercury, 1958) and 'My Blue Heaven' (Mercury, 1959).

dots A fairly neutral term for printed notation, *dots* becomes mildly disparaging if there is a suggestion that a musician is *only* able to play from dots – i.e. is unable to improvise.

double time The practice of 'superimposing eight beats at

medium tempo over four beats to the bar at slow tempo'
(Lyttelton [2], 123) was an important component in the improvising style of pianist Art Tatum and has subsequently become
a widely employed device, particularly useful for perking up a
slow ballad.

Down Beat   The leading American jazz magazine, founded in
Chicago in 1933.

Dreamland   The Dreamland Café was one of the main jazz
venues in *Chicago* during the early years: 'That Dreamland was
some place,' said Alberta Hunter. 'It was *big* and always packed'
(quoted in Shapiro, 94). The young Lil Hardin (later Lil
Armstrong) had a band there; in 1921, she joined King Oliver
and his Creole Jazz Band, who also played at Dreamland in the
days before Louis Armstrong arrived from *New Orleans* in
1922.

drums   The insistent percussion of early jazz was frequently
viewed with critical amusement or distaste, and it is true that
bands such as the *ODJB* invited this by emphasising the comic
aspects of a drum-kit augmented with kitchen impedimenta.
Thereafter, the sophistication of jazz drumming developed as
rapidly as other aspects of the music, the key figures being
Warren 'Baby' Dodds, who played with Oliver and Armstrong,
and Ellington's long-serving drummer Sonny Greer. The stylistic revolution of the 1940s caused some problems, when *bebop*
soloists found themselves pitted against drummers – often excellent musicians on their own terms – whose rhythmic vocabulary
was less advanced: a Norman Granz session which teamed
Charlie Parker with Buddy Rich is sometimes cited as evidence
of this. But the post-war period saw the emergence of some
outstanding drummers, including Max Roach and Art Blakey,
who are more than equal to the challenges of bebop and after.
Less welcome, perhaps, is the frequent appearance of lengthy
drum solos in live (and sometimes recorded) performances
which, given their lack of harmonic or melodic possibilities, are
really only of interest to fellow-percussionists, while the rest of
us count the bars.

Duke[1]   Edward Kennedy 'Duke' Ellington (1899–1974), by
some distance the greatest composer/bandleader in the history
of jazz, and a superb if reticent pianist too. 'The truly recognisable Ellington sound,' wrote Peter Gammond, 'materialised

towards the end of 1927 when the band was coming to the end of a long stay at the Kentucky Club on New York's 49th Street' (sleevenote to *Hot from Harlem*, World Records, 1979); for over half a century, Ellington's band was unquestionably the best in the business. Although opinions inevitably differ as to which Ellingtonian vintage was finest of all, many listeners would cast their vote for the early 1940s line-up which included trumpeters Rex Stewart and Cootie Williams; trombonists Lawrence Brown and Joe Nanton; clarinetist Barney Bigard; saxophonists Harry Carney, Johnny Hodges and Ben Webster; and a rhythm section comprising Fred Guy (guitar), Jimmy Blanton (bass), Sonny Greer (drums) with, of course, the Duke himself on piano: a representative collection of recordings from this period is *In a Mellotone* (RCA Victor). As a pianist, Ellington, like Earl Hines (see *Fatha*), provides a bridge between the Harlem *stride* piano of James P. Johnson and the post-*bebop* modernism of Thelonious *Monk*, each of whom he could abruptly and disconcertingly resemble: recordings which usefully illustrate this range include the two solos 'Black Beauty' and 'Swampy River' (Okeh, 1928), the trio dates collected as *Piano Reflections* (Capitol, 1953) and the late quartet – Ellington, Joe Pass (guitar), Ray Brown (bass), Louis Bellson (drums) – on *Duke's Big Four* (Pablo, 1973).

Duke Ellington's compositions range from indestructable standards like 'Black and Tan Fantasy', 'Rockin' in Rhythm', 'Mood Indigo', 'Solitude', 'Take the "A" Train' and 'Perdido' to extended works like *Black, Brown and Beige*: transcending jazz, they place him among the dozen or so major American composers. 'It Don't Mean a Thing (if it ain't got that swing)', written by Ellington and his manager Irving Mills, was a sensational success when recorded by his 'Famous Orchestra', with its inimitable vocal by Ivie Anderson and distinctive *wah-wah* brass (Brunswick, 1932), providing a motto and a name for the *swing* era which followed it. And as for 'the truly recognisable Ellington sound': '"You know," said André Previn, "another bandleader can stand in front of a thousand fiddles and a thousand brass, give the downbeat, and every studio arranger can nod his head and say, 'Oh yes, that's done like this.' But Duke merely lifts his finger, three horns make a sound, and nobody knows what it is!"' (*From Satchmo to Miles*, 64).

Duke[2] There is (as I remark elsewhere in these pages) only one Duke; but another who deserves mention is Duke Jordan, the pianist on those incomparable *bebop* ballads – most famously,

'Embraceable You' – recorded by the Charlie Parker Quintet
for Dial in 1947. A later trio session (Vogue, 1954) established
him as a distinctive composer and soloist who remains underrated.

Eagle Band Led by Frankie Dusen, the Eagle was among the most prominent bands in *Storyville*; around 1912, it numbered both Sidney Bechet and Bunk Johnson among its members.

Earl There are many Earls and *King*s in jazz (but only one *Count* and one *Duke*). For Earl Hines, see *Fatha*; of the rest, perhaps the most interesting is *alto* saxophonist Earl Bostic, who moved on from the *bebop* scene of 1940s *52nd Street* to lead a commercially successful band, scoring a major success with the resonantly evocative 'Flamingo' (King, 1951).

East Coast In the 1950s, the *cool* style of the *West Coast* was countered by the more astringent hard bop of the East Coast. Given the geographical mobility of jazz musicians, and their propensity to form improbable musical alliances, both terms are of limited value.

Ebony Concerto Stravinsky's major contribution to jazz-influenced music was commissioned by Woody Herman, written for Benny Goodman, and completed in 1946.

Ella Although – or because – Ella Fitzgerald is the most successful vocalist in the history of jazz, her work has often been regarded with sneering suspicion by critics: 'Miss Fitzgerald's singing gives the impression of a subtly veneered surface unsupported by any solid wood,' wrote Jack Cooke, in a not especially ill-disposed review (*Jazz Monthly*, 6:11, January 1961, 24) at the time when her popularity was at its highest and her critical reputation at its lowest. Born in 1918, she was singing with the Chick Webb Orchestra by the time she was in her late teens, and she took over nominal leadership of the band when Webb died in 1939, having already achieved an early success with the re-worked nursery song 'A-Tisket, A-Tasket' (Decca, 1938). Her jazz integrity, like Louis Armstrong's and Billie Holiday's, was somewhat compromised by her long association with American Decca, who tended to present these artists in commercial, gimmicky contexts – in Ella Fitzgerald's case, most famously with The Ink Spots in the million-selling 'Into Each Life Some Rain Must Fall' (Decca, 1944); later, from the mid-1950s onwards, she recorded for Norman Granz a sequence of 'Songbook' albums, mostly featuring large studio orchestras with string sections, which equally failed to endear her to jazz purists. But the purists were depriving themselves of some notable pleasures: in *The George Gershwin Songbook* (Verve, 1959), for instance, Nelson Riddle's arrangements provide the lush setting for some outstanding interpretations (such as the heart-stopping last verse of 'The Man I Love'); while *Like Someone in Love* (Verve, 1957), arranged and conducted by Frank DeVol, is a still more persuasive collection of *standard songs*, including some ambitiously off-beat examples. Ella Fitzgerald's more straightforward jazz work is probably best sampled in her numerous recordings with the Tommy Flanagan Trio, her regular accompanists for several years, with whom she recorded such memorable 'live' albums as *Ella in Hamburg* (Verve, 1965). She continued singing and touring until well into her seventies; she died in June 1996. 'To hear her,' wrote Colin MacInnes, 'is to be given, in the most telling and pleasurable form, that particular lift of the spirits that is the great gift of jazz, in its more positive moods, to our frowning, cross-patch age' (*England, Half English*, 134).

electro-jazz   A self-explanatory term, describing the usually unfortunate process of adding electrically amplified rock instruments to jazz. It has its admirers, however, and according to Phil Johnson, Miles Davis's *In a Silent Way* (Columbia, 1969) and *Bitches Brew* (Columbia, 1970) are 'seminal texts in the great electro-jazz crossover experiment of the late-Sixties and Seventies' (*Independent*, 20 March 1996).

Empress   The 'Empress of the Blues' is Bessie Smith (1898–1937), for Panassié 'far away above any other female blues singer', an 'incomparable artist' of 'monumental simplicity – yet with a strain of pathos and an astonishing swing' (Panassié, 227). All this is true; and she had, besides, the kind of life and death which – like Billie Holiday's or, for that matter, Sylvia Plath's – rapidly transforms a career into myth. It 'could be briefly described as "rags to riches … to rags"' (*JOR* [1], 282). Born in Chattanooga, Tennessee, her reputation remained local and her voice unrecorded until 1923, when she began a prolific and highly successful recording association with Columbia (a test session for Okeh, featuring the equally unknown Sidney Bechet, had been rejected). After 1930, her career swiftly and steeply declined, and she made her last records in 1933. She died following a road accident. According to John Hammond (*Down Beat*, November 1937), she was refused admission to a Mississippi hospital on grounds of her colour; although this version of events has been refuted by Chris

Albertson in 'The Death of Bessie Smith' (*PBJ*, 78-88), it seems ineradicably fixed in the collective jazz consciousness, and the likelihood of some medical confusion or inefficiency remains.

Esquire[1] A US magazine which in the mid-1940s sponsored the eponymous All-American Jazz Band and annual jazz concerts. The latter were notable for their striking and sometimes unlikely combinations of outstanding musicians: for instance, in the second concert (17 January 1945), Billie Holiday appeared with the Duke Ellington Orchestra (and the master of cereminies was Danny Kaye). These concerts were an obvious forerunner of Norman Granz's *Jazz at the Philharmonic* series.

Esquire[2] A UK jazz record label, founded in 1948, by the bandleader, drummer, record collector and jazz entrepreneur Carlo Krahmer; among its earliest performers was the 21-year-old Johnny Dankworth, playing *clarinet* in a quartet led by Vic Feldman (who was then fourteen years old). For the next two decades, it provided an important outlet for British jazz (and *skiffle*) and for important American recordings – including those of John Coltrane, the *MJQ*, Thelonious *Monk* and Sonny Rollins – from, among others, the Prestige and New Jazz labels.

Ethiopian Melody See *Old Folks at Home*.

Famous Door   The Famous Door was one of the most celebrated jazz clubs on *52nd Street*, 'whose name derived from an old door it had which was covered with autographs' (Clarke, 244); it was also the name of a jazz record label founded by former Keynote producer Harry Lim in 1972.

Fatha   Earl 'Fatha' Hines was a pianist and bandleader, whose career, like *Duke* Ellington's, embraced virtually the whole history of jazz, from *ragtime* to post-modernism. The nickname is self-explanatory: as Alun Morgan puts it, 'Quite simply, Earl was the father of keyboard jazz as we know it today' ('Piano Man', BBC Radio 3, 2 October 1995). In 1928, at the age of 23, he succeeded Lil Armstrong as pianist with the Hot Five/Seven and recorded the most famous duet in jazz history, 'Weather Bird' (Okeh, 1928), with Louis Armstrong. In the same year his own band began a long residency at the Grand Terrace club in Chicago, recording for Decca (1934–5) and RCA Victor (1939–40). He was 'the most influential jazz pianist of the thirties and forties' (Hardy, 361), but like some of his contemporaries he suffered a partial eclipse in the 1950s, re-emerging as a major soloist in the 1960s; notable work from this period includes such albums as *Spontaneous Explorations* (Contact, 1964) and *Tour de Force* (Black Lion, 1972). He continued to perform until shortly before his death in 1983.

Fats   Various portly musicians have earned this nickname, including the trumpeter Fats Navarro and the rhythm and blues singer Fats Domino, but its unchallenged rightful owner is Thomas 'Fats' Waller (1904–43). In a music characterised by passionate and even rancorous disagreements, Waller divides listeners' opinions with unusual sharpness: many regard him as something of a buffoon, insufferably cheerful and minimally talented. According to Max Harrison, he 'is probably the saddest case of ill-spent talent which jazz on records can show' (*JOR* [2], 297); and it is true that the recordings by 'Fats Waller and his Rhythm' made for RCA Victor during the 1930s are both repetitive and, in their nostalgic dependence on already outmoded piano techniques, anachronistic. On the other hand, his music (in smallish doses) can give real pleasure, while as a composer Waller produced such indestructible standards as 'Ain't Misbehavin'' (1929), 'Honeysuckle Rose' (1929), 'My Very Good Friend the Milkman' (1929) and 'Handful of Keys' (1933). Donald Clarke's assertion that 'Nobody did more than Fats Waller, except Louis Armstrong himself, to bring jazz to popular music' (Clarke, 237) is fair enough, but by the same token he brought popular music to jazz and arguably diminished it.

Feetwarmers A name adopted by several bands, from the *New Orleans* group led by Sidney Bechet in the 1930s to John Chilton's British revivalists of the 1970s: 'The suggestion is of a band guaranteed to keep the extremities in rhythmical action' (*Jazz A–Z*, 93).

field-holler See *work-song*.

52nd Street The post-war jazz club centre of New York is celebrated in Thelonious *Monk*'s suitably energetic 1948 composition '52nd Street Theme'. It was the focal point for musicians on the East coast, with a notably relaxed approach to *sitting in*: 'When you'd go down the Street at night,' says Shelley Manne, 'you'd go into one place and hear somebody, and play; and then you knew another set was going on someplace else, you'd go over there' (quoted in Gitler, 140); these places included the Downbeat, the *Famous Door*, the Hickory House, *Kelly's Stables*, the Onyx, the *Spotlite* and the Three Deuces. But 52nd Street's unique place in jazz was not to last. Ahmed Basheer recalls meeting Charlie Parker there in 1954: he 'came walking down 52nd Street with a contemplative air, like he was passing through a ghost town. He looked at The Deuces, The Onyx, all the clubs he used to play, and they were all strip joints. Just a ghost town' (quoted in *Bird: The Legend of Charlie Parker*, 33).

Five Pennies The Five Pennies (of whom there could be up to fourteen) was the best-known of the many recording bands led by trumpeter Red Nichols from the mid-1920s onwards. Others included the Arkansas Travellers, the Charleston Chasers, the Red Heads, and Red and Miff's Stompers: these names, Nichols said, 'were usually just last-minute thoughts at the completion of a session (we sometimes did as many as ten and twelve a week), often designed to preserve the anonymity of the musicians' (quoted in Shapiro, 270).

flare up Panassié defines this as 'A note held by a player at the end of a chorus to lead the band into a final collective improvisation' (Panassié, 85), and cites Armstrong's 'Willie the Weeper' (Okeh, 1927) as an example.

Flat Foot Floogie A spoof dance invented by Slim Gaillard as a successful novelty hit in 1938, 'Flat Foot Floogie' was re-recorded by him in a version which also featured Charlie Parker and *Dizzy* Gillespie (Bel Tone, 1945); it thus has the peculiar distinction of featuring equally in the histories of kitsch popular music and of *bebop*.

flatted Same as *flattened*, in phrases such as *flatted third*, fifth, seventh etc.

flute The *flute*, as Leonard Feather observes, 'has been obliged virtually to gate-crash its way into jazz acceptance' (*BOJ*, 141–2). This may be in part due to its lack of 'a flexibility compa-rable to the vocal technique of the Negroes' (Panassié, 85) but the main reason is its restricted range and colour: consequently, it has figured mostly as a contrasting second instrument for saxo-phonists or, in the case of Roland Kirk, one item in a whole musical ironmongery. In the 1950s the flute found a home among the cooler textures of *West Coast* jazz, especially in the hands of Bud Shank: Alan Zeffert notes that 'his flute sound is, perhaps, the most "authentic" in jazz and his technique is flaw-less' (*JOR* [2], 257).

Flying Home Lionel Hampton's 1939 composition 'Flying Home' was the great *swing* hit of the early 1940s, performed and recorded by him on numerous occasions (e.g. RCA Victor, 1940; Decca, 1942).

form The two basic forms of jazz are the twelve-bar *blues* and the 32-bar AABA *standard song*; but these are merely starting-points for a limitless field of musical exploration. As Leonard Feather has rightly asserted, 'Jazz can be played in four-four time, waltz time or any other time' (*BOJ*, 8); and it can be based on absolutely any harmonic or thematic material. If you want to invent a jazz version of the *Marseillaise* or the *Peer Gynt* suite or the 'March of the Siamese Children' from *The King and I*, go ahead: each has, anyway, been done already. But jazz's flexi-bility does not mean that it can dispense with form or structure, even though this myth often prevails among people who should know better. This morning (10 November 1996), an experi-enced and presumably not unintelligent broadcaster (Peter Hobday), professing a fondness for jazz on BBC Radio 3, said he considered jazz an 'anarchic form of music' and the phrase 'the discipline of jazz' an oxymoron. Nothing could be further from the truth: jazz, like poetry, is usually most disciplined when it sounds most free. To improvise successfully over chords demands a precision of harmonic thinking not possessed (because not needed) by most classical musicians, while jazz ensemble playing requires no less exactness than a string quartet, even though it may lack the latter's full notation and sustained rehearsal. Of course, many inexperienced jazz musicians – again, like poets – persuade themselves that they can improvise freely without first mastering the formal disciplines of their art; but Robert Frost's famous observation that 'writing free verse is like playing tennis with the net down' is every bit as applicable to *free jazz*.

foxtrot Newton points out that 'the invention of new rhythmic dances became a minor industry' in the early years of the century and that the 'crop of 1910–15, Turkey Trot, Bunny Hug, etc., produced the most lasting formula, the Foxtrot' (Newton, 48). For jazz, the significance of this phenomenon is twofold: firstly, the enthusiasm for novel dance crazes, which continued into the 1920s, exactly preceded and thus informed the increasingly close connection between jazz and commercial dance music in the inter-war years; secondly, the foxtrot made viable and brought into circulation an enormous number of the *standard songs* which, after the *blues*, were to become the major source of material for jazz musicians.

Frankie and Johnny This song, known in St Louis in the 1880s and probably dating from as far back as 1840, is significant because, as Leonard Feather says, 'structurally it has the classic twelve-measure format of the blues ... with the first four bars on the tonic and the next on the chord of the subdominant, and so on through the regular 1-4-5-1 blues pattern'; Feather notes that this harmonic formula 'was common in American folk music of both races a century ago' and that the 'twelve-measure form can even be found in English and French balladry as far back as the thirteenth century' (*BOJ*, 13).

free jazz An improvisatory, atonal form of jazz principally associated with the *alto* saxophonist Ornette Coleman. 'In the Ornette Coleman Quartet of the late 1950s, the musicians created their own harmony as they went about their business of collectively improvising melodies – he calls this "harmolodics", but at the time it was known as "free jazz"' (Linton Chiswick, *Independent*, 22 September 1995). *Free Jazz* is in fact the title of a notable or notorious album (Atlantic, 1960), by the augmented Ornette Coleman Quartet (the additional musicians are Eric Dolphy, Freddie Hubbard, Scott LaFaro and Ed Blackwell), which has produced polarised reactions in its listeners. As Charles Hamm judiciously puts it: 'To ears conditioned to traditional jazz, or traditional music of any kind, this music is chaos. To ears that can listen in other ways, it is a fascinating and exciting collage, rich in detail, that changes with each hearing, depending on which instrument or instruments one listens to most closely' (quoted in Tirro, 345). That looks reasonable enough, though the latter part of it is as true (or, aguably, truer) of a string quartet by Beethoven or Schubert as it is of Coleman's music. Max Harrison describes this 38-minute improvisation as 'quite unsurpassed for its beauty and affirmation, its spontaneity and organic development' (*JOR* [2], 51); Philip Larkin, however, noted that *Free Jazz* 'bears on its sleeve a reproduction of a Jackson Pollock painting, and until the last 10 minutes or so of its 40-minute length is a fair musical representation of it, a patternless reiterated jumble' (Larkin, 204). Dexter Gordon once accused his fellow *tenor* player Ronnie Scott, who for a while dabbled with the style, of playing 'all that free shit'; but Scott replied: 'I don't play free. I play very *cheaply*, but I don't play free' (quoted by Steve Voce, *Independent*, 27 December 1996).

front-line   Those players of wind instruments who in a small jazz band usually stand or sit in front of the *rhythm section*: in a genuine *New Orleans* band, these instruments were traditionally *clarinet, cornet* (later, *trumpet*) and *trombone*; from the mid-1920s onwards, members of the saxophone family – especially *alto* and *tenor* – became increasingly important.

funky   In established English slang *funk* is 'cowardice, terror', but in Black use *funky* is 'sweat generated during sex' or 'the odour of the female genitals' (Green, 104); unsurprisingly, the latter usages are the ones which inform the jazz sense of these words. 'The word "funk",' says Donald Clarke, 'originally referred to strong smells – there was a club in New Orleans called the Funky Butt – and meant "low-down" or "gutbucket" in music' (Clarke, 347). By the 1950s, however, 'funky' had come to have much the same musical connotations as 'raunchy' – sexy, soulful, with a powerful yet laid-back after-hours feeling. Charlie Parker's 'Funky Blues' (Clef, 1952) is a perfect example and an altogether momentous track: it features both Parker and

Johnny Hodges which, as Lord (Grey) Gowrie memorably puts
it, 'is like having Rembrandt and Velasquez to dinner' ('The
Tingle Factor', BBC Radio 4, 26 September 1995). In the early
1960s, the element of *soul* became more dominant: Berendt
describes the Cannonball Adderley Quintet as 'one of the most
renowned combos in modern funk- and gospel-inspired music'
(Berendt, 156). In an enjoyably tetchy 1961 review (the culprit,
or victim, was Ray Bryant), Alun Morgan complained: 'The
"party line" at the time of writing is gospel-soul-funk, or something; whatever the name, it has given me some embarrassing
hours of listening' (*Jazz Monthly*, January 1961, 21).
Subsequently, the earlier meanings have resurfaced, albeit in an
excitably imprecise way: 'it's the urban jazz funk dance party ...
Pee Wee Ellis on bar-walking funk tenor ... [Maceo] Parker,
the godfather of funk saxophone ...' (John Fordham, *Guardian*,
25 April 1994). 'Funky' always implies, in a sense which need
not be at all pejorative, a lack of finesse and sophistication: 'The
words "elegant" and "funky" don't splice well' (Nick Coleman,
Independent, 24 February 1996).

G **ate**   Barry Ulanov records this as 'once upon a time synonymous with jazz musician; used as well to designate Louis Armstrong or Jack ("Big Gate") and Charlie ("Little Gate") Teagarden' (Ulanov, 95). As with Armstrong's more famous nickname, *Satchmo*, the reference is presumably to his mouth: a 'gatemouth' is '(US Black use) a gossip, a loudmouth' (Green, 107).

Gennett   The record label of the Starr Piano Company, Richmond, Indiana, is important in the history of jazz for two reasons: in 1918, it was 'the first label to break the monopoly of Victor and Columbia' (Priestley, 2) in producing shellac 78s; while in 1923 King Oliver's Creole Jazz Band made for Gennett the momentous sides which included, in 'Chimes Blues', the first recorded solo by Louis Armstrong (Gennett's British licensee, Edison Bell, apparently didn't consider these tracks worth issuing).

Georgia   Like many other state and place names in the southern USA, *Georgia* is used more for its evocative resonance than for any more precise geographical reason: for instance, among the members of the Georgia Jazz Band, who recorded with *Ma* Rainey in 1926, only Fletcher Henderson came from Georgia (Buster Bailey was from Memphis, Charlie Green from New Orleans, Coleman Hawkins from Missouri); while Sidney Bechet's lovely 'Georgia Cabin' (RCA Victor, 1941) is a warmly nostalgic down-south mood piece. Georgia's most famous and enduring representation in jazz, and in popular music generally, is undoubtedly Hoagy Carmichael's 1930 composition 'Georgia on my Mind', recorded by practically everyone from Louis Armstrong (Okeh, 1931) to Ray Charles (ABC-Paramount, 1959).

gig   A one-off engagement at a specific venue, as opposed to a continuing residency, is a *gig*: precisely why is unclear, though Middle English *gigge* provides both the horse-drawn carriage and the whirligig, with their respective (and perfectly appropriate) connotations of travel and rushing about.

gobstick   An early, disrespectful nickname for the jazz *clarinet*.

gone   The surprisingly logical, inevitable consequence of being 'sent': see *send*.

Gramercy Five The name of two distinct small groups drawn from the otherwise largely uninteresting *swing* band of Artie Shaw: the first, in 1940, comprised Bill Butterfield (trumpet), Johnny Guarnieri (harpsichord), Al Hendrickson (guitar), Jud DeNaut (bass) and Nick Fatool (drums); the second, in 1945, included Roy Eldridge (trumpet), Dodo Marmarosa (piano), Barney Kessell (guitar), Morris Rayman (bass) and Lou Fromm (drums). As these personnels indicate, the Gramercy Five forms an intriguing bridge between swing and *bop*; the earlier group's recording of 'Summit Ridge Drive' (RCA Victor, 1940) was a notable commercial success.

groove Any particularly soulful or *funky* number: 'an exultant Latin groove by Joe Henderson' (Phil Johnson, *Independent*, 4 October 1994). The usage derives from the shellac or vinyl gramophone record: to be *in the groove or to groove along with* is to empathise with the music to the extent of being *sent* by it. Like several other jazz terms, 'groove' – especially in its adjectival form 'groovy' – has suffered the fate of being by turns extremely *hip* and unforgivably *square*. Jonathon Green reports that, having meant 'delightful, wonderful, pleasant, enjoyable' in the 1960s, 'groovy' had come by the early 1980s to mean 'passé, out of date' (Green, 124). Its subsequent, somewhat equivocal rehabilitation is tinged (like that of 'fab') with more than a hint of campness.

growl 'A deep, rough tone produced with the lips on wind instruments in imitation of tones used by blues singers' (Panassié, 96), the growl was especially favoured by musicians of Ellington's *jungle* period such as Bubber Miley and Joe 'Tricky Sam' Nanton.

guitar On the face of things it seems odd that the instrument inextricably associated with the *blues* should occupy so marginal a position in jazz. In fact, the guitar was present in early jazz bands, but it was somewhat ironically superseded by the more incisive-toned *banjo*, which was better able to hold its own with the strident brass textures of *New Orleans* music; for exactly that reason, however, the banjo was out of place in the orchestral jazz which evolved during the 1920s, in which the guitar gradually made its modest reappearance. This hesitant progress was followed by two further crises of identity: the first in the 1930s, when the need for amplification in *swing* bands produced the electric guitar, and the second in the post-war *rock 'n' roll* era, when the guitar became primarily identified with a quite distinct kind of music.

Unsurprisingly, this background has made the guitar's role in jazz far less clear-cut than that of the other main instruments and has also provoked a fundamental disagreement about just how the guitar should sound. Blues musicians apart, the most celebrated guitarists in jazz are Eddie Lang, best known for his work with violinist Joe Venuti and for his guitar duets with Lonnie Johnson, according to whom he 'could play guitar better than anyone I knew' (quoted in Shapiro, 266); *Django* Rheinhardt, who switched from pre-war acoustic to post-war electric; and Charlie Christian, the great swing era player who used an electric guitar. It was Christian who pioneered the use of the guitar as a single-note solo instrument; Barney Kessel recalls that in 1937 the black musicians he was working with, who had all heard Christian, would tell him: 'Play like a horn.' At that point Kessel couldn't understand 'that they meant to play a melodic single-note line, to try and play and sound like a tenor saxophone or trumpet' (quoted in Gitler, 42).

gutbucket   A style of 'earthy, slightly ribald music that made much use of wah-wah mutes and "growl" techniques' (Lyttelton [1], 164), popular in *Harlem* around 1924. 'Bubber [Miley, the leading exponent of these techniques] used to say, "If it ain't got swing, it ain't worth playin'; if it ain't got gutbucket, it ain't worth doin'"' (Duke Ellington, quoted in Shapiro, 235). Gutbuckets were used in *barrelhouses* to catch the drips, or gutterings, from faulty taps and leaky barrels.

Hackensack   The Thelonious *Monk* number
'Hackensack' (Prestige, 1954) was named in honour of
the great jazz recording engineer Rudy Van Gelder and
his studio at Hackensack, New Jersey; it is a version of Monk's
'Lady Be Good' *riff*, sometimes called 'Rifftide'.

Hamp The nickname of Lionel Hampton (b.1913), who 'gave
the vibraphone its identity as a jazz instrument' (*JOR* [2], 121),
and who also led a highly successful big band, formed in 1940.

Harlem Along with *New Orleans*, *Chicago* and – a little later
– *Kansas City*, Harlem, New York, is among the legendary
homes of jazz: 'By 1900 Harlem was already becoming the
biggest black city on earth' (Clarke, 99). But it also shared with
New Orleans that element of cultural diversity and synthesis
which is so important to jazz: it was, in Rex Harris's dated but
otherwise accurate phrase, 'an exclusively Negro yet nevertheless cosmopolitan community'. Harris goes on to spoil things,
however, by grumpily adding: 'Harlem, in fact, has never
produced a jazz band, but the superficial swing of the white
commercial world was echoed in the Cotton Club and the dance
halls of the New York Negroes' (Harris, 166). Though this is
misleading – or arguable only from Harris's very
specifically purist viewpoint – the suggestion that Harlem
provided a waiting and welcoming audience for jazz is valid
enough.
    Marshall Stearns notes that 'the peak of jazz intensity moved
from Chicago to New York in the mid 'twenties' (Stearns, 131).
This was centred on two initially separate but soon intercon-
nected phenomena, neither of which would have quite satisfied
Harris's notion of a 'jazz band': one was the Harlem *stride* piano
school, including such figures as James P. Johnson, Willie 'The
Lion' Smith and, by this time, youngsters such as *Fats* Waller
and *Duke* Ellington; the other was the emergence of the big
band which was to change the nature of jazz during the coming
decade. Stearns lists some of the New York bands of the mid-
1920s: Fletcher Henderson's from 1923, Sam Wooding's at the
Club Alabam in 1925, Cecil Scott's in 1926, Chick Webb's at
the *Savoy* Ballroom in 1927, and many others. 'Harlem was
honeycombed with hot spots' (Stearns, 132) – among them, the
Cotton Club, where Duke Ellington's orchestra opened in
1927, and *Connie's Inn*, where Louis Armstrong appeared in
the Fats Waller/Andy Razaf show *Hot Chocolates* in 1929. 'The

world's most glamorous atmosphere,' was Ellington's reaction on first seeing Harlem: 'Why, it is just like the Arabian Nights!' (quoted in Clarke, 161).

Harlem Footwarmers   Probably the best-known of several aliases used by the ever-resourceful *Duke* Ellington in the late 1920s: 'We were signed with Victor,' he explained, 'but we'd wax for other companies as the "Jungle Band", "Joe Turner and his Men", "Sonny Greer and His Memphis Men", and the "Harlem Footwarmers"' (quoted in Shapiro, 229).

Harlem Hamfats   A successful studio band of the late 1930s, the *Harlem Hamfats* were in fact *New Orleans* musicians based in *Chicago*, featuring an Armstrong-influenced trumpeter and vocalist, Herb Morand.

harmolodics   See *free jazz*.

hat   A *hat* is a mute: 'the trumpets and trombones, often in hats …' (Claude Thornhill, quoted in Gitler, 251).

Hawk   See *Bean*.

head   The opening (and, often, closing) arrangement of a theme, excluding any extended improvisations, when this is arrived at in rehearsal rather than being pre-arranged and notated: a 'head arrangement', says, Ulanov, is 'a score put together on the spot, by members of a band' (Ulanov, 95); '"Leapin' at the Lincoln" was a head arrangement of Gershwin's "Lady Be Good"' (Clarke, 218).

hep   According to a 1939 'Vocabulary of Swing Terms', a *hep-cat* is '(1) a swing devotee who is "hep" or alert to the most authoritative information' or '(2) a swing musician' (*PBJ*, 135); see also *hip*.

Herd   Three big bands led by Woody Herman in the 1940s and 1950s were known respectively as the First, Second and Third Herd: they were among the most successful fusions of *swing* band scale with elements of *bebop* thinking, memorable for their high proportion of able soloists and for justly famous set pieces such as Stan Getz's 'Early Autumn' with the Second Herd (Capitol, 1948). Herman's First Herd, so named by George Simon of *Metronome*, was formed in 1944, but Simon comments: 'As far back as 1939 we were referring to his band as "The Herd"' (quoted in Gitler, 188).

hi-de-ho   Familiar from the vocal refrain of 'Minnie the Moocher', this term describes the kind of novelty number common in the *swing* era and specifically associated with Cab Calloway: 'All he was concerned with,' says Milt Hinton, 'was that we play this music, and it was all hi-de-hos – "Minnie the Moocher", and "Smokey Joe", and "Reefer Man" and what not' (quoted in Gitler, 57).

high hat   The *high hat* (or hi-hat or sock cymbal) is a pedal-operated pair of cymbals: the lower remains stationary while the upper moves up and down, striking against it.

hip   Of all the definition-resistant words in this book, *hip* is the most cheerfully recalcitrant of them all, 'an uncrackable code ... devised to defend the cat's quick kernel from the rip-off' (Carr, 11). The inward, illicit side of jazz was always hip, but the word itself acquired its potently evasive sense only in the 1940s or early 1950s: Lester Young is perhaps the major jazz figure to embody it, as the authors of *The Hip* imply. It is closely related to *cool* jazz and to *beat* writing; its spirit informs the dress-sense as well as the music of the post-war jazz modernists and achieves its graphic representation in the marvellous 1950s LP sleeves of labels such as *Blue Note*, Contemporary and *Verve*. Its most famous representatives in jazz are *Chet* Baker and Gerry Mulligan – stylish, iconoclastic, and deeply troubled – while outside jazz it embraces key fifties icons from James Dean to Jack Kerouac. Despite this, the hip never loses the cachet of its minority, cognoscenti appeal: if, by some mischance, a hip record or book or film becomes a popular success, either its hipness is terminally compromised or (which is much more likely) the joke is on the wider public, who have parted with their gratefully received money but really don't quite know what it's all about.

hokum   The use of peculiar accessories to produce musical or merely ridiculous effects was known as a *hokum deal*. At the relatively sensible end of this scale were the various items of headgear employed as *mutes*; but John Steiner mentions several much odder objects. Phil Dooley, for instance, 'had a trapeze above his drums, loaded with a variety of kitchenware and, on each end, a "kitty" or donation pot', while Jasper Taylor 'found a way to tune and play melody on a bedspring'; this, says, Steiner, was arguably 'the most hokumized item of all' (Hentoff, 161–2). Adrian Rollini in the late 1920s 'invented two oddities called the goofus and the hot fountain pen' (*BOJ*, 143). The unusual instruments – including *manzello, stritch*, and a variety of whistles – in the musical armoury of (Rahsaan) Roland Kirk may arguably count as more recent examples of hokum. Jazz in general, despite being dismissed in its earlier days as a form of novelty music, has been remarkably restrained in this matter, mostly confining itself to a core of respectably orthodox instruments even when the music performed on them has been neither respectable nor orthodox.

The *Hokum Boys* was a partnership of blues singers – Georgia Tom, Tampa Red and Big Bill Broonzy – who performed 'comic, self-guying songs with country overtones and urban expression' (*JOR* [2], 106); Tampa Red also played and sang with the Hokum Jug Band.

Holiday, Billie See *Lady Day*.

honky-tonk A *honky-tonk*, like a *barrelhouse*, was a modest and probably disreputable *New Orleans* dive; though the term carries a distinct air of sexual euphemism (rather like 'hanky-panky'), it derives from the clangorously out-of-tune pianos to be found in such places – though, oddly, the honky-tonk piano would subsequently acquire a kind of middlebrow respectability in the hands of a performer such as Winifred Atwell.

hoofer A tap-dancer, often featured in jazz club performances of the 1920s and 1930s.

hook See *riff*.

horn Any brass or reed instrument – and sometimes, anachronistically, other instruments too – can be described as a *horn*; *The Horn* is the title of a jazz novel by John Clellon Holmes.

hot Capturing the brashly exuberant flavour of early *New Orleans* jazz, with its brass-heavy *front line* and its close links with *marching bands*, 'Hot connotes the emotional warmth and intensity of the music, and has come to stand for the peculiar brand of intonation, phrasing, "attack", and vibrato which characterize this style of jazz' (Berendt, 10). The *trumpet* (or, especially in earlier jazz, the *cornet*) is potentially the hottest of instruments; and the open, extrovert music of Louis Armstrong in the 1920s is as unmistakably hot as that of Miles Davis – muted, introspective – is *cool*: Philip Larkin plausibly described Armstrong's recording of 'St Louis Blues' (Okeh, 1929) as 'the hottest record ever made' (Larkin, 230).

Unsurprisingly, the original OED is innocent of a musical context for 'hot', which does however appear in the *Supplement*: 'Applied to elaborated dance music and playing of the virtuoso kind; also to the performer'; the first attestation, similarly referring to 'hot dance music' rather than 'jazz', is from the *Gramophone* in 1928. The definition is predictably prim but also subtly misleading, while the citation is significantly late, given that the 'classic period of Armstrong Hot Five and Hot Seven recordings' (*JOR* [1], 15) had begun in 1925 and by 1928 was drawing to its close. The *Oxford Companion to Music* is even more quaintly cautious: 'It appears that the terms *Straight Jazz* (or *Sweet Jazz*) and *Hot Jazz* apply respectively to jazz played as written and jazz in which the extempore element is prominent. The difficulty of attaching a definite significance to such terms is, however, considerable, as the practitioners of this branch of the musical art, and their journalistic following, do not seem to use them at all precisely' (Scholes, 537).

During the 1920s, the word naturally found its way into the names both of bands – Louis Armstrong's Hot Five (and Hot Seven), Jelly Roll Morton's Red Hot Peppers – and of individual compositions: Armstrong's 'Hotter than That', Duke Ellington's 'Hot and Bothered', Fletcher Henderson's 'Hot Mustard'. Even by 1928, however, 'hot' was beginning to lose something of its original urgency: the excellent Ellington number, recorded by a band which was large and sophisticated enough to call itself an 'Orchestra' (Okeh, 1928), takes it to mean fast and frantic rather than distinctively brass-led; it is already a long way from New Orleans. A British studio group of the 1930s, the Six Swingers, recorded jazz medleys under the title 'Hot Pie'.

Later applications of 'hot' could be thoroughly inaccurate. The all-string line-up of The Quintet of the Hot Club of France (violin, guitars, bass) was, despite the undoubted talents of Stephane Grappelly and *Django* Reinhardt, by definition scarcely lukewarm. This adds a degree of mischievous irony to the moment in Cole Porter's 'Now You Has Jazz' (from the film *High Society*) at which Louis Armstrong assures Bing Crosby: 'The Frenchmans all / Prefer what they call / *Le jazz hot*' (Capitol, 1956).

Humph Entries for jazz nicknames in this book are otherwise confined to a handful of major American musicians, but Humphrey Lyttelton is an exception to every rule. This civilised old-Etonian iconoclast, 'one of the very few first-class traditional trumpet players to be born in England' (*JOR* [1], 219), led the revivalist band which recorded a famous clandestine set with Sidney Bechet while he was on a strictly non-performing visit to England (Melodisc, 1949); during the 1950s Lyttelton steered his band on a fascinating if dangerous course into the *mainstream*, of which the turning-point is perhaps the album *Humph at the Conway* (Parlophone, 1954); since then, he has continued to perform in a variety of contexts – including notable duets with Buck Clayton and reworkings of Ellington and Mercer songs with the former teenage pop singer Helen Shapiro – while developing parallel careers as journalistic, author and broadcaster. His books which share their main title with his radio programme *The Best of Jazz* are among the most engagingly intelligent ever written on the subject.

Improvisation Jazz is commonly described as an improvised music: indeed, one of the commonest ways in which early critics conveyed their displeasure at its vaguely anarchic barbarity was to insist on just this point. But the music of *New Orleans* was carefully structured and tightly arranged, and the great 'improvised' solos themselves were often reverently copied note for note. As orchestral jazz developed in the 1920s, arrangers such as *Duke* Ellington and Don Redman became as influential in shaping the course of the music as the performers they wrote for; while the spectacularly imaginative improvisers of the *bop* era often based their work on the chord sequences of especially challenging *standard* tunes. The great jazz improvisations, in fact, occur when an outstanding performer is given the space – a chorus or more – to create an individual masterpiece within an intensely if unobtrusively disciplined framework.

intro An *introduction*, usually of two or four bars, preceding the opening statement of a theme.

ivories The keys of the *piano* and thus the piano itself: 'to tickle the ivories' is to play the piano – see *tickler*.

Jack the Bear   Around the turn of the century, John 'Jack the Bear' Wilson was the most celebrated of the piano *ticklers*: his legendary status in the history of New York jazz is somewhat akin to that of *Buddy Bolden* in *New Orleans*, and he is memorialised in a Duke Ellington composition named after him.

jam   An improvised performance, involving several *front-line* musicians, using a predetermined chord sequence but not otherwise arranged. The jazz usage seems to occur by analogy with other meanings: the superimposition of one sound on another, as in radio jamming, or the close proximity of several objects jammed together; a connection with preserve-making is seductive but fanciful, despite the existence of a number called 'Clarinet Marmalade'.

   The OED's earliest citation of the word's jazz connotation is a thoroughly obtuse passage from the *Melody Maker* in January 1929: 'There are many variations on this rhythm – which make excellent breaks – or "jams" as they now call them when they are taken by the whole band, the word "break" being used only when it is intended to signify that it is played by one instrument or a section moving together or unaccompanied.' But *Fortune* (August 1933) gets the right sense: 'The jazz musicians' jam sessions where the players vie with one another in hot solos'. That element of competitiveness is essential: a *jam session* is an occasion for aggressive virtuosity rather than for delicate introspection. Mezz Mezzrow recalled the informal get-togethers of musicians at 222 North State Street, Chicago: 'I think the term "jam session" originated right in that cellar' (quoted in Shapiro, 131). According to Barney Kessel, there are three things to be gained from jam sessions: firstly, the 'social camaraderie'; secondly, 'learning tunes, learning things and hearing how other people played'; and thirdly, 'feeding your own ego and flexing your own egotistical musical muscles' (quoted in Gitler, 26).

   The word occurs less often than other jazz terms in titles, and when it does it tends to have a punning or humorous sense, as in Artie Shaw's 'Traffic Jam' (RCA Victor, 1940), with its cacophonous imitation of motor-horns, or Duke Ellington's 'Jam-a-Ditty' (Musicraft, 1946), pronounced to rhyme with 'humidity'. Slim Gaillard's 'Slim's Jam' (Bel Tone, 1945) purports to recreate a session in which musicians including *Dizzy* Gillespie and Charlie Parker wander in and take solos, while Gaillard provides instructions such as 'We're in A-flat' and 'You take the next chorus'. Though of some historical

interest (not least for Parker's spoken complaint that he's having
'a little reed trouble'), this is plainly all a joke, and by the early
1950s the word 'jam' had begun to sound thoroughly uncool.

jazz The OED's main definition flounders as follows: 'A kind of
ragtime dance ... hence the kind of music to which this is danced;
(the usual sense) a type of music originating among American
Negroes, characterized by its use of improvisation, syncopated
playing, a regular or forceful rhythm often in common time, and
a "swinging" quality ... loosely, syncopated dance music.' This
is not very useful, though it is instructive in its dependence on
terms which imply that jazz is something outlandish, alien and
hostile to the European musical tradition: 'ragtime', 'improvisation', 'syncopated'; precisely the same emphases will be found
in the introductory section to the *Oxford Companion to Music*'s
entry on jazz (Scholes, 534–5). As entries elsewhere in these
pages make clear, jazz evolved from a far more complex and
cosmopolitan fusion of cultural influences than the compilers
of such standard reference books cared to contemplate: see, for
instance, *Creole, New Orleans*.

'The very word "jazz" entered print and printable meaning
... around 1915,' as Francis Newton says (Newton, 2-3);
'Clarence Williams claimed to be the first to use the word on
sheet music around 1915, when he described "Brown Skin, Who
You For?" as "Jazz Song"' (Clarke, 68), and at about the same
time *Lamb's Café* in *Chicago* displayed a banner bearing the
words 'Jazz Band'. Frank Tirro has unearthed one slightly earlier
and rather eccentric printed reference, to a baseball team
'trained on ragtime and "jazz"', in the San Francisco *Bulletin* of
6 March 1913 (Tirro, 51). Its previous history – unprinted,
unprintable – has been long been a subject of entertaining if
fruitless conjecture: jazz is a Creole corruption of French *jaser*
(to chatter or gossip); it is derived from the name of Jasbo or
Jazzbo Brown, a singer and dancer, or of the Jazzbo Band; it is
(like *rock*) a black slang term for sexual intercourse; it is
onomatopoeic, suggesting energy and excitement. It is, of
course, probably all these things and many more; for the apparently conflicting etymologies are in reality mutually reinforcing,
cross-fertilising ones. Barry Ulanov mentions another 'character', apart from Jasbo Brown, 'who may or may not have been
a part of jazz in the nineteenth century: one Charles Alexander
or Charles Washington from Vicksburg, Mississippi, whose
name was shortened to make *Chas* or *Chaz*, then perhaps *Jass*
or *Jazz*' (Ulanov, 89): in his incarnation as Charlie Alexander,

it is surely he who is wryly invoked by Louis Armstrong as a long-lost friend – one who conveniently shares his name with the band's pianist – in the spoken introduction to 'When It's Sleepy Time Down South' (Okeh, 1931). Even the more exotic suggestions recorded by David Boulton (*PBJ*, 117–8) – that a wind quartet called Razz's Band somehow metamorphosed into Jazz's Band or that the word began as Portuguese *dios*, travelled East as *joss* (as in 'joss stick') and thence became jazz via a Chinese colony in San Francisco – needn't be completely dismissed: a Razz's Band or a 'Frisco Joss Band might very easily have found its name involuntarily modified once jazz was in the air.

At first, the word was often spelt 'jass' rather than 'jazz', as in the original name of the Original Dixieland Jass Band; according to H. O. Brun, the spelling was changed from 'ss' to 'zz' by the *ODJB* 'because children, as well as a few impish adults, could not resist the temptation to obliterate the letter "j" from their posters' (Lyttelton [1], 14). This is likeable but unlikely. Arnold Loyacano's more pedestrian recollection also seems more plausible: it was, he said, in Chicago that 'people started calling our music "jazz". The way the northern people figured it out, our muic was loud, clangy, boisterous, like you'd say, "Where did you get that jazzy suit?" meaning loud or fancy. Some people called it "jass". Later, when the name stuck, it was spelled was a "z", "jazz"' (quoted in Shapiro, 88).

Tirro rightly reminds us that 'Jazz was not the only style to emerge just before World War I, for the music of Schoenberg, Bartók, and Stravinsky was in formative stages too' (Tirro, 171). This presents the temptation (which Tirro resists) of viewing jazz as a facet of the modernist movement, emerging concurrently not only with those three composers but with the painting of Picasso, the fiction of Joyce, the poetry of Pound. But the analogy won't hold, for two principal reasons. One is that jazz was a synthesis of disparate elements achieved by a large number of mostly black and mostly obscure American musicians; the fully achieved masterpieces of the great individual talents – Armstrong or Ellington or Parker – were to come later on. The other is that the time-scale of jazz is so foreshortened in comparison with that of the other arts: indebted though it undoubtedly was to earlier music, it was nevertheless a new form rather than an old one experiencing a periodic overhaul. If there was a revolution in jazz at all comparable to modernism in the other arts, it would not occur until the mid-1940s: see, for instance, *bebop, modern*.

In Britain, jazz was described, without enthusiasm, in *The Times* of 19 January 1919: a jazz band, it said, is 'one of the many American pecularities that threaten to make life a nightmare' and its object 'is to provide as much noise as possible' (quoted in Godbolt, 3). Nevertheless, jazz – misrepresented and misunderstood as it may have been – rapidly became something of a craze in Britain: this was partly due to the interest created by the extended visit of the ODJB, from April 1919 until July 1920, but Jim Godbolt rightly notes some of the related phenomena which immediately preceded it. These included: the first recording, in January 1919, by a British group claiming to be a jazz band, 'All Bound 'Round with the Mason-Dixon Line'/'That Moaning Trombone' by Murray Pilcer and his Jazz Band (Edison Bell, 1919); an advertisement for 'Jazzin' the Jazz' (with the Brazilian Trio led by Captain T. Jackells of Shoeburyness!) in the *Performer* of 23 January 1919; and the music publisher Darewski's advertisement of 'Great Jazz Hits' in *Era*, 12 February 1919 (Godbolt, 6). The word may not have entered print until 1915; but in England, by the spring of 1919, it was being printed a great deal.

Nevertheless, the term remained abundantly misunderstood. Many listeners persisted in thinking it synonymous with dance music, a confusion reinforced by the fact that many British jazz musicians earned their steadier incomes playing with *dance bands*. The reaction of George Melly's prep-school headmaster in the late 1930s was typical of a generation and a class. At the announcement on the radio of some innocuous item by Ambrose or Roy Fox, he would 'attempt to silence the set before the first note', as Melly recalls in his wonderfully entertaining memoirs: 'If, as usually happened, the switch came off in his hand, he would drown the music, as he fumbled to replace it on its axle, by shouting "filthy jazz!" at the top of his voice' (*Owning-Up*, 10).

Jazz Age 'It was an age of miracles, it was an age of art, it was an age of excess, and it was an age of satire,' wrote F. Scott Fitzgerald, in 'Echoes of the Jazz Age' (*The Crack-Up*, 10). Fitzgerald defined the *Jazz Age* as lasting from May Day 1919 until October 1929: he was not, of course, 'particularly interested in the music' but in 'a state of mind' (Stearns, 111). His definition does, however, make a sort of musical sense, spanning as it does the time from jazz's arrival as a fashionable if not quite respectable form of music to its next major point of transition – the cross-fertilisation with *dance bands* which occurred

at the end of the 1920s, heralding the *swing* era. Noting that
'jazz' and 'dance music' were interchangeable terms for much
of the American public, Donald Clarke adds: 'The less strict
moral atmosphere of the 1920s, in which young women went
out dancing with their young men friends without supervision
(and smoked cigarettes, and bobbed their hair!) carried the same
association: hence the "jazz age"' (Clarke, 123–4). Reviewing
the four-volume LP set *Thesaurus of Classic Jazz* (Philips, 1961),
Philip Larkin commented: 'This is the music of the Jazz Age,
but the Jazz Age did not really like jazz' (Larkin, 19). It preferred
the 'bright, skilful, melodic, but slightly bloodless music'
produced by orchestras such as Paul Whiteman's and Jean
Goldkette's.

Although Scott Fitzgerald's interest was not primarily in the
music, he was nevertheless capable of satirising its more pretentious aspects. The orchestra, apparently of symphonic size, at
one of Gatsby's parties performs 'Mr Vladimir Tostoff's latest
work, which attracted so much attention at Carnegie Hall last
May'; it is called 'Vladimir Tostoff's Jazz History of the World'
(*The Great Gatsby*, 56). The allusion is to Paul Whiteman's
Aeolian Hall concert performance of Gershwin's *Rhapsody in
Blue*.

Jazz at the Philharmonic A series of concerts organised by
Norman Granz between 1944 and 1957 on much the same principle as many of the sessions for his Clef, Norgran and *Verve*
record labels: i.e. to assemble a group of star musicians, more
or less irrespective of their compatibility, and allow the chem-
istry between them to work (or not). Critics have often been
rather sniffy about this: André Hodeir, for instance, squarely
blames a 'mediocre performance' by the unlikely combination
of Benny Carter and Oscar Peterson not on the musicians themselves but on 'the man who brought them together, deliberately
neglecting that indispensable unity for the sake of publicity: I
am referring to Norman Granz' (*Toward Jazz*, 76).
Nevertheless, JATP, like his other enterprises, produced its fair
quota of successes and, no less important, provided gainful
employment for some outstanding performers in difficult times;
Granz 'made more jazz available in public and on record than
any other individual' (Clarke, 324).

Jazzbo Panassié offers the singer Jazzbo Brown as an 'improbable' source of the word *jazz* (Panassié, 127); it seems likelier
that the performer took his name from the music, as did the

Jazzbo Band, an unrecorded American group who visited Britain in 1918, a year before the *ODJB*.

Jazz Messengers   Drummer Art Blakey founded the Jazz Messengers in 1954, and since then the group has nurtured several generations of talented jazz soloists. The original personnel comprised Kinny Dorham, Hank Mobley, Horace Silver, Doug Watkins and Blakey himself; later group members in the 1950s included Jackie McLean, Johnny Griffin and Junior Mance. During the following decade, the outstanding edition of the Jazz Messengers was the one which featured Freddie Hubbard, Wayne Shorter and Curtis Fuller: this is the personnel heard on a memorable album recorded at the Renaissance Club in Los Angeles, *Three Blind Mice* (United Artists, 1962). Blakey's more recent protégés have included Keith Jarrett and Wynton Marsalis.

jazz-set   Godbolt notes that 'drum-kits used to be known as "jazz-sets"' (Godbolt, 4), presumably on the rather odd assumption that only jazz musicians use drums.

Jazz Singer   *The Jazz Singer* (1927), starring Al Jolson, was the first successful talking picture, but apart from its title it had nothing to do with jazz.

Jelly Roll   Ferdinand 'Jelly Roll' Morton was 'the Chopin of jazz' (*JOR* [1], 230). 'Born into a New Orleans creole family of French-Spanish-African descent in 1890, Morton is now universally accepted as the first great jazz composer,' writes Dave Gelly (*Observer*, 17 September 1995), while Martin Williams calls him 'the first great master of form in jazz (Williams, 17). For Williams, Morton's music represents 'an alliance between ragtime and the blues, with importations from French and Spanish folk musics, Baptist hymns, and martial music' (Williams, 21), a concoction of those disparate ingredients from which *New Orleans* jazz was blended. Morton had no doubts about his own importance – 'I invented jazz in 1902,' he said (Berendt, 7) – but not everyone found this self-confidence endearing: 'Sure Jelly Roll Morton has talent,' Duke Ellington conceded, 'talent for talking about Jelly Roll Morton' (Mick Hamer, *Listener*, 26 March 1981). His distinctive nickname had nothing to do with the piano: like 'jazz' itself, 'jelly roll' – 'the female genitals' (Green, 152) – is an instance of the music's cheerfully subversive appropriation of black sexual slang. Gregory R. Staats (*PBJ*, 90) cites the 'New Jelly Roll Blues' (1927) of Peg Leg Howell:

> I never been to church and I never been to school,
> Come down to jelly I'm a jelly-rollin' fool,
> I got a sweet jelly to satisfy my worried soul,
> I like to have my jelly and I like to have my fun.

'Ain't Gonna Give Nobody None of My Jelly Roll' is a standard of the New Orleans repertoire, composed by Clarence Williams and Spencer Williams, and dating from 1919.

Morton's recordings with the Red Hot Peppers (Victor, 1926–8) are generally regarded as jazz classics; while towards the end of his life (1885–1941) he made an immense and extraordinary series of recordings for the Library of Congress (1938), described by Francis Newton as 'the most impressive single document of New Orleans jazz' (Newton, 57). More manageable and still more affecting are a dozen titles he recorded late the following year – autumnal revisitations of numbers such as 'King Porter Stomp', 'Winin' Boy Blues', 'The Naked Dance' and 'Buddy Bolden's Blues' (Commodore, 1939).

jig   Quite apart from its commonplace musical meaning – 'a lively dance usu. in 6-8 time; a dance tune of like kind' (Chambers) – *jig* has a typically interlocking cluster of senses bearing on jazz. Jig, or 'jigaboo', is a 'derog. term for a Black person' (Green, 153), while 'jig-a-jig' (like '"Jug Jug" to dirty ears') is sexual intercourse. 'Jigs', puzzlingly plural here, 'had long been a US slang term for negro, and the word … was used in many song titles,' says Jim Godbolt, adding the nice instance of Louis Armstrong's recording of 'Just a Gigolo' (Okeh, 1931) in which he 'impishly changes one of the lines in the lyric to "Just a Jig I know"' (Godbolt, 189). Jig's Club, in Wardour Street, the leading London jazz club of the 1930s and 1940s, was 'probably the most frequented of the West End "dives" by white jazz buffs' (Godbolt, 190); its house band recorded 'live' at the club in 1941 for Regal-Zonophone.

jive   This meaningless-looking word has acquired an assortment of meanings – from faking to dancing – and the one most relevant to jazz modulates from almost-serious in the *swing* era ('the language of swing' [*PBJ*, 136]) to wholly frivolous in the post-war world of *bop* ('comic speech, usually larded with ambiguous jazz terms' [Ulanov, 96]); for an example of the latter, see *voot*.

joint   Any venue, especially a lively one: 'The joint, as Fats Waller would have said, was jumping' (James Baldwin, *Another Country*, 16).

jug   An amateur, impoverished form of jazz group, consisting of players unable to afford orthordox instruments, was the *jug band*: apart from empty jugs, the instrumentation, made from easily-found utensils, might typically include *kazoo, washboard* and tea-chest *bass*. This homely assemblage formed the basis of *skiffle*.

The Louis Armstrong title 'Knockin' a Jug' conceals a different story. It was recorded for Okeh early on the morning of 5 March 1929 in New York by a *pick-up* band comprising Armstrong, Jack Teagarden, Happy Cauldwell, Joe Sullivan, Eddie Condon and Kaiser Marshall. They had been working the previous evening and so, as Marshall recalled, 'we didn't bother going to bed; I rode the boys around in my car in the early morning hours and we had breakfast about six so we could get to the studio at eight. We took a gallon jug of whisky with us.' Asked for the number's title by the studio manager, Armstrong 'looked around and saw the empty jug in the middle of the floor and said, "Man, we sure knocked that jug – you can call it 'Knockin' a Jug'." And that's the name that went on the record' (quoted in Shapiro, 275). It's a story which neatly catches the spirit, in more than one sense, of jazz recording throughout much of the shellac era; the other title from that session, 'I'm Gonna Stomp, Mr Henry Lee', vanished without trace.

jukebox   The jukebox – an 'electrical coin machine which plays records' (Ulanov, 96) – is most commonly associated with pop music of the 1950s and 1960s, but it had already played an important part in jazz. Martin Williams notes, for instance, that the early recordings of Billie Holiday, made in the mid-1930s, 'were primarily intended for an urban black audience, and during those depression years they sold largely to jukebox operators' (Williams, 80). The accompanists on these jukebox sessions would typically comprise a *pick-up* group drawn from the finest big bands: there were no rehearsals, few retakes, and the material was often bland, but these haphazard encounters between talented musicians could produce astonishingly good results. The word 'jukebox' itself 'probably comes from the Gullah "juke" or "joog", meaning "disorderly" or "wicked"'

(Clarke, 230) and seems to have been in use by the time Walter
Roland recorded 'Jookit Jookit' (Vocalion, 1933).

jump To *jump* is to *swing*, and the word consequently became
common in the titles of up-tempo swing numbers – 'One o'Clock
Jump', 'Jump, Lester, Jump', and so forth. 'For me,' said Billy
Ternent, 'the first hearing of Smack's [Fletcher Henderson's]
band was a thrill I shall remember as long as I live. The *jump*
that this band had was simply amazing' (quoted in Shapiro,
215). But 'jump music' also took on a more specific meaning
as the wildest facet of the swing era, whose main characteristics, according to the authors of *The Hip*, were 'breakneck
tempos fast enough to outdistance the roadrunner; more self-
mocking humour than a season of *Bilko* re-runs; and lyrics so
hip they're almost surreal – as in "Plant ya now, an' dig you
later!"' (Carr, 29). Clarke puts the matter more calmly: 'A jump
band was a small group that combined the beat and the drive
of the big jazz band with the repetitious chorus associated with
the blues, in effect making something new of the Swing Era's
predilection for riffs' (Clarke, 272). The energy and the surre-
alism provide a partial bridge from swing to *bebop*.

jungle The *jungle style* – 'a name reflecting the tastes of the all-
white night-club audiences who got a thrill out of any suggestion
of African primitivism' (Russell Davies, *Listener*, 20 January
1983) – was devised by Duke Ellington for his *Cotton Club*
orchestra in 1927: 'Ellington created his "jungle style" with
[Bubber] Miley and [Joe] Nanton. The expressive growl sounds
of trumpet and trombone reminded listeners of voices moaning
in a jungle night' (Berendt, 50). A more recent use of 'jungle'
to designate a variant of West Indian reggae is another matter
altogether: '"Jungle-style music" was an expression occasionally used by jazzmen, but it had little to do with the aggressive,
slightly sinister, macho style of jungle today' (Nicholas Bagnall,
Independent on Sunday, 20 November 1994).

Kansas City   Like *New Orleans* and *Chicago*, Kansas City became a focal point for jazz musicians and gave its name to a musical style; and, as with *Storyville* in New Orleans, the reason was at least partly political. The key figure was Tom Pendergast, 'boss of the Democratic party in Kansas City from 1927 to 1938', who 'encouraged gambling and night life; clubs as such appeared during his years of power in vast proliferation, and all had music of one sort or another' (Franklin S. Driggs, 'Kansas City and the Southwest', in Hentoff, 195). Marshall Stearns quotes pianist Sammy Price's comment, 'There was no Depression for the gangsters', and adds: 'The gangsters were doing well and the jazz bands got jobs' (Stearns, 135). Pendergast was convicted for tax evasion in 1938, since when, Driggs drily notes, 'relatively little of importance has occurred' – with the startling exception of Jay McShann's band of 1942, including Charlie Parker.

The Kansas City style, which developed during Pendergast's creatively corrupt reign, is distinguished by a 'preference ... for ensemble riffs or solos backed by riff accompaniment' (Panassié, 143); the main bands associated with it are those of *Count* Basie, Andy Kirk and Benny Moten. Reviewing an album of Moten reissues from the late 1920s, Sinclair Traill noted that 'The K.C. bands had assimilated the barrel-house piano music' and that this combination 'produced a strong, very rhythmic beat entirely suitable for the many big dance halls supported by the large Negro population' (*Jazz Journal*, February 1965, 35). The young Charlie Parker's Kansas City apprenticeship had lasting effects: '"Now's the Time" [is] a blues with obvious roots in the Kansas City riff music of Parker's youth' (Harrison, 19).

Kaycee   'Kaycee' and 'K.C.' are both common abbreviations for *Kansas City*: 'In those years around 1930, Kaycee was really jumping ... In Kaycee, nothing mattered' (Mary Lou Williams, quoted in Shapiro, 278).

kazoo   Although the *kazoo*, found in *jug* and *skiffle* bands, is properly a 'cigar-shaped tube containing a parchment membrane which vibrates when the instrument is blown' (Panassié, 143), the noise it makes is indistinguishable from that of comb and paper, by which its is sometimes replaced.

Kelly's Stables   A *Chicago* club owned by Bert Kelly, closed in 1930. For its last six years, 'Johnny Dodds, New Orleans clarinet genius, led a small band there' (*Jazz A–Z*, 144): it was a group of four musicians, according to Tommy Brookins, and 'No one had a fixed salary but the tips were such that they used to make between a hundred and twenty-five and a hundred and seventy a week' (quoted in Shapiro, 118). Later, there was a Kelly's Stables in New York, on *52nd Street*.

Kentucky Club A *New York* venue, whose special significance in jazz history is that it provided the meeting-point for *Duke* Ellington and his future manager Irving Mills. 'The first time I heard Duke Ellington was at the Kentucky Club in New York,' Mills recalled, adding that, when he had heard 'Black and Tan Fantasy', 'I immediately recognised that I had encountered a great creative artist – and the first American composer to catch in his music the true jazz spirit' (quoted in Shapiro, 230). Because of this, Mills built his next show at the *Cotton Club* around Ellington and increased the size of the band from five to ten pieces.

Kid Edward 'Kid' Ory (1886–1973) was a notable trombonist who played with Louis Armstrong's Hot Five, wrote 'Muskrat Ramble' (1926), retired from music in the 1930s and resurfaced in the *New Orleans* revival of the early 1950s; but his more crucial importance is as one of jazz's great enablers. For between 1913 and 1919, when he left New Orleans for Los Angeles, Ory's 'sidemen included some of the most notable musicians of New Orleans – Johnny Dodds, Jimmy Noone, King Oliver, and Louis Armstrong' (Tirro, 166). 'The first time I remember seeing Louis Armstrong, he was a little boy playing cornet with the Waifs' Home band in a street parade,' said Ory. 'Even then he stood out' (quoted in Shapiro, 60). The man who talent-spotted *Satchmo* would have earned his place in jazz history even if he never played a note.

King There are many Kings in jazz – the earliest was *Buddy Bolden*, often called King Bolden – but the name inalienably belongs to Joe 'King' Oliver (1885–1938): 'cornet player, mentor of Louis Armstrong, and musical director of the Creole Jazz Band, the finest jazz ensemble of its day' (Tirro, 163), he 'hit Chicago in 1917 and for the next eight years or so he was the undisputed King of Jazz anywhere in America' (Harris, 94); according to Tommy Brookins, 'There was no other orchestra during that time that could play like Joe Oliver and his Creole Jazz Band' (quoted in Shapiro, 104). Like *Kid* Ory, he employed the finest musicians available: Armstrong, Paul Barbarin,

Barney Bigard, Sidney Bechet, the Dodds brothers, Jimmy Noone and Ory himself among them. 'King Oliver and Louis,' said Buster Bailey, 'were the greatest two trumpeters I ever heard together' (quoted in Shapiro, 108).

It was during their 1923 residency at the Lincoln Gardens, Chicago, that King Oliver and his Creole Jazz Band recorded prolifically: 'Within the space of eight months in 1923 were waxed thirty-seven titles for four different record labels, Paramount, Gennett, Okeh, and Columbia' (Harris, 97); these are among the most important historical documents in jazz. In the late 1920s Oliver's career went into a steep decline: he was dogged by ill-health, poverty, and simple chronological bad luck – jazz was moving towards the *swing* era, while his pre-eminence in *New Orleans* music had passed to his own erstwhile second cornet-player, Louis Armstrong.

Nat 'King' Cole (1919–65) was an influential jazz pianist and trio-leader from 1936 to 1948 who subsequently became an immensely successful singer of popular ballads such as 'Mona Lisa' (Capitol, 1950) and 'When I Fall in Love' (Capitol, 1957).

kitchen department   An unflattering nickname for the *rhythm* section in general and specifically for the *drums*.

klook   The nickname of drummer Kenny Clarke is short for 'klook-a-mop', a nonsense term imitative of offbeat drum accents which gained a sufficiently wide currency to be included in Tom Lehrer's parody of the 'cool school' in 'Clementine' (Decca, 1959).

Koko   This Charlie Parker number (Savoy, 1945), based on the chord sequence of Ray Noble's 'Cherokee', is arguably the most striking and famous of all *bebop* transformations: 'I was working over "Cherokee,"' said Parker, 'and, as I did, I found that by using the higher intervals of a chord as a melody line and backing them with appropriately related changes, I could play the the thing I'd been hearing' (quoted in Shapiro, 342-3). 'Cherokee' itself had already been the basis of a legendary Sunday after-noon *jam* session at the New York's Heat Wave club in 1944 at which, somewhat improbably in view of Earl Bostic's subse-quent career, the 'two horns were Bird and Bostic. Both of them were great and had a great feeling towards each other' (Hal Singer, quoted by Gitler, 76).

Ko-Ko   Not to be confused with the almost identically-titled Charlie Parker piece, this is an equally important *Duke*

Ellington piece, its definitive version recorded for RCA Victor in 1940: 'In "Ko-Ko",' says Martin Williams, 'Ellington's talent reaches a full expression'; the final variation, he adds, 'is one of the most richly orchestrated moments in all of Ellington and all of jazz' (Williams, 108–9). For André Hodeir, 'it constitutes the most perfect example of Duke Ellington's language (then at the height of its development) and remains one of the undisputed masterpieces of orchestral jazz' (*Toward Jazz*, 26). But Hodeir's admiration for the 1940 recording is contrasted with his disgust at Ellington's remake of the piece for his generally well-regarded *Historically Speaking* LP (Bethlehem, 1956) in a five-page comparative analysis which is among the most passionate in jazz criticism.

Lady Day Billie Holiday (1915–59) – called 'Lady Day' by the 'President', or *Pres*, Lester Young – 'was the supreme jazz singer' (*JOR* [2], 136). 'I named him the "President",' she said, 'and he named me "Lady", and my mother "Duchess". We were the Royal Family of Harlem' (quoted in Shapiro, 302). She was fortunate in her early association with exactly compatible musicians such as Young, *Count* Basie, and Teddy Wilson: her recordings with them for Columbia between 1935 and 1942 are justly regarded as among the major documents of jazz, as are the two harsher-sounding sessions for Commodore in 1939 and 1944 (which include the Columbia-rejected 'Strange Fruit', her most famous single track). Her contract with American Decca from 1944 had the consequences usually associated with this label (cf. Louis Armstrong, *Ella* Fitzgerald): the jazz interest was compromised by popular material and bland studio arrangements, but her public grew accordingly. By 1952, when she joined (almost inevitably) Clef/Verve, her voice was technically deteriorating, yet her copious later recordings with outstanding small groups (and even with strings) have an earned melancholic wisdom spiced with wry humour – the moon over foggy London town shining 'upside-down' – which make them, for me, superior to her early work and indeed to any other singing in jazz; for Martin Williams, too, 'the frayed edge of her sound in her later years seems to come from a deeply suppressed sob which, if she ever let go, would bring tears she might never be able to stop' (Williams, 86).

Although there are some great *blues* performances in Billie Holiday's work – her version of 'Billie's Blues' from the 1944 *Esquire* concert, with interjections from Louis Armstrong, is a masterpiece – it was as a re-inventer of *standard songs* that she equalled and in emotional depth surpassed the more formally accomplished Ella Fitzgerald. Three years before her death, she published her autobiography, *Lady Sings the Blues*, ghosted by William Dufty, but nevertheless memorable at least for its very striking first paragraph: 'Mom and Pop were just a couple of kids when they got married. He was eighteen, she was sixteen, and I was three' (*Lady Sings the Blues*, 5).

Lamb's Café This was the *Chicago* venue whose owner, Smiley Corbett, sent for the white Tom Brown's Band in 1915: 'Soon a banner over the door of Lamb's Café read "Jazz Band"' (John Steiner, in Hentoff, 148). This may have been the first such public display of those momentous words.

Latin   The geographical position and cultural history of *New Orleans* meant that there was a Latin-American – often called simply *Latin* – influence on jazz from its earliest days. In New Orleans music, elements of the *tangana* or, as *Jelly Roll* Morton called it, the 'Spanish tinge' seem natural and unforced; and there is a strong Latin presence too in the ubiquitous south-of-the-border dance numbers of the 1930s. Such assertive rhythmic patterns were less easy to combine with the complexities of *bebop*, however: although Norman Granz was fond of placing musicians such as Charlie Parker and *Dizzy* Gillespie in Latin contexts in the early 1950s, the effect tends to be of an exotic and imperfectly-assimilated mannerism, rather like the equally fashionable Indian influence on pop music a decade or so later.

Leadbelly   The nickname of Huddie Ledbetter (1885–1949): Paul Oliver describes him as 'a giant in American folk-lore' who was 'a blues singer and much else besides' (*JOR* [2], 175). That 'much else' suggests a career which veered more towards folk than to blues, and it is not entirely fanciful to view him as the link between *Blind Lemon* Jefferson and Bob Dylan.

Leroy's   In the 1920s, this was 'the most prestigious venue for Harlem pianists' (Lyttelton [2], 35) such as James P. Johnson and Willie 'The *Lion*' Smith; it was here that the former introduced young *Fats* Waller to the latter, and soon they 'were roaming the Harlem piano haunts together, a triumvirate of invincible keyboard masters' (Lyttelton [2], 36).

lick   A *lick* may be a *break* or a *riff* or any other fairly concise musical idea: 'used in the early days to designate a phrase or a solo' (Ulanov, 96).

Lighthouse   Bass-player Howard Rumsey's jazz club at Hermosa Beach, California: 'Most of the West Coast's finest musicians have worked and recorded at the Lighthouse' (*JOR* [2], 249), usually under the banner of Howard Rumsey and his Lighthouse All-Stars – a particularly celebrated incarnation of which included Bud Shank, Bob Cooper and Max Roach (Contemporary, 1954).

Lion   Pianist Willie 'The Lion' Smith has been rather sourly called 'one of the best-known comedians in jazz' (*JOR* [1], 286), but he is also one of its great chameleons, adept at styles from *stride* to *mainstream,* and admired by both *Duke* Ellington and Billy Strayhorn, who described his style as 'a strange mixture of counterpoint, chromatic harmony and arabesque-like figures as refreshing to the ears as spring-water to the lips' (quoted in *JOR* [2], 271). It was apparently James P. Johnson (whom he in return named 'The Brute') who gave him his nickname, although he also claimed that he had wanted to become a rabbi and 'Because of my devotion to Judaism, I was called "The Lion of Judah", later abbreviated to "The Lion"' (quoted in Shapiro, 177). A snappy dresser and a powerful personality, he 'would stride into a club growling a warning: "The Lion is here"' (Clarke, 161).

Lippy According to Willie 'The *Lion*' Smith, 'The three of us, "The Lion", "The Brute" [James P. Johnson], and "Filthy" [*Fats* Waller], plus a guy called "Lippy", used to run all over town playing piano' (quoted in Shapiro, 171). The 'guy called "Lippy"' was Raymond 'Lippy' Boyette, one of the legendary piano *ticklers*: 'Lippy was said to be able to ring anybody's doorbell in the middle of the night, saying, "It's Lippy, and I've got James P. with me", and gain immediate entrance' (Clarke, 162).

liquorice stick A liquorice (or in its US spellings licorice or licorish) stick is, for obvious reasons of colour and shape, a *clarinet.*

Little Jazz The nickname of trumpeter Roy Eldridge, regarded by some listeners as the link between Louis Armstrong and *Dizzy* Gillespie.

Livery Stable Blues Recorded by the *ODJB* in 1917, 'Livery Stable Blues' – 'an improvisation on the 19th-century religious ballad "The Holy City"' (Priestley, 20) – was the number which alerted Buster Bailey and other *Memphis* musicians to improvised, *New Orleans* jazz. When it was used to open Paul Whiteman's *Aeolian Hall* concert, it was 'introduced apologetically by Whiteman "as an example of the depraved past from which modern jazz has risen"' (Clarke, 107).

longhair The jazz *aficionado*'s contemptuous term for lovers of classical and other serious music is an example of tactical misalignment, for both should surely be united against their common enemy – the reductive idiocy of pop music. The usual grouch of the dim and indolent about much contemporary music – that it is harmonically and rhythmically incomprehensible – is, after all, just as applicable to *modern* jazz as it is to other forms of composition.

Louisiana   The former French territory, including the *Mississippi* delta, in which jazz originated: 'Most of the slaves imported into the Southern states of the USA were West Africans, the French (in whose Louisiana territory jazz first emerged) having a special preference for slaves from Dahomey' (Newton, 29). Francis Newton also points out that African culture, and specifically African music, survived in a purer form in the French zone than elsewhere in the USA: for instance, officially sponsored voodoo drum-dances still took place in New Orleans as late as the mid-1880s. 'However, Negro music rapidly began to fuse with white components, and the evolution of jazz is the result of the fusion' (Newton, 30).

Louisiana Five   This authentic-sounding name masked a group of white musicians, including trombonist Tom Brown, who was 'the first white musician to bring New Orleans jazz to Chicago' (Tirro, 177–8); they recorded for Columbia in 1919.

lowdown   A notable instance of the sort of jazz word which exudes connotation and evades definition, *lowdown* is an 'expression applied above all to the blues, and particularly to slow blues which call for a "lowdown' interpretation whether by a singer or instrumentalist' (Panassié, 153). But that tells us less than we might guess from the word itself, which implies a relaxed, intuitive inwardness with the music – in contemporary terms, 'laid back' is part of it. Duke Ellington's 'New Orleans Low-down' (Vocalion, 1927) is a loping, straightforward twelve-bar *blues* (with some nice *wah-wah mute* work by Bubber Miley); while the vocalist in 'Doin' the New Low-Down' (Okeh, 1928) – he is Ellington's manager Irving Mills, who would occasionally insist on singing – commends the lowdown, which had inevitably been transformed into a dance for the revue *Blackbirds of 1928*, as a 'crazy thing' with a 'lazy swing'.

Ma Gertrude 'Ma' Rainey (1886–1939), 'the mother of the blues', was 'one of the most influential blues singers of the age' (Tirro, 131), whose 'relation to the "classic" blues is approximately the same as Jefferson's is to the country blues' (*JOR* [1], 263). Her recording career, mostly for Paramount between 1923 and 1929, was brief but prolific, and included work with Louis Armstrong, Coleman Hawkins, Fletcher Henderson, Kid Ory and Don Redman; like many other jazz pioneers, she died in virtual obscurity.

Magnolia 'The fashion was for something elaborate and nostalgic,' writes George Melly (*Owning-Up*, 19), explaining how the band with which he sang in the 1950s came to be called Mick Mulligan's Magnolia Jazz Band. Its music may not have lasted particularly well, but the name is wonderful, while Melly himself is one of the British jazz scene's (and the human race's) more conspicuous assets.

Mahogany Hall 'The largest of the cabarets on Basin Street' (Spencer Williams, quoted in Shapiro, 23), Mahagony Hall was owned by Spencer Williams's aunt, Lulu White; hence, Williams's composition 'Mahogany Hall Stomp', recorded on several occasions by Louis Armstrong.

mainstream A rather more precise and useful term than it at first appears, *mainstream* entered jazz currency in the 1950s: 'When the new term "Mainstream" was coined in England for the Swing style of the present, Buck Clayton became – certainly among European jazz fans – one of the leading personalities of Mainstream jazz' (Berendt, 134-5). It defined a music which was already well-established and which has continued to thrive: the small-group, acceptable face of *swing*, proving that, between the historically momentous styles of *New Orleans* on the one hand and *bebop* on the other, jazz had retained a life outside the big bands.

Jazz audiences, of course, are notoriously partisan; I suspect this may be especially true of British audiences, which is possibly why they also develop other passionately irrational allegiances – for instance, to scruffy and inept football teams. Francis Newton in 1959 noted that 'Mr Humphrey Lyttelton, who has been brave enough to change his band from a "traditionalist" to a "middle period" [i.e. mainstream] unit, is engaged in interminable polemics with former members of his public who regard this change as treasonable' (Newton, 184). Musicians them-

selves tend to be less bothered by such unnecessary segmenta-
tion, and to them the mainstream has proved as broadly
hospitable as its name suggests: that admirable and ubiquitous
drummer Sid Catlett, for example, was as at home when playing
with mainstream-modernists like Coleman Hawkins or Lester
Young as he was with New Orleans pioneers such as Louis
Armstrong or Sidney Bechet (he recorded with all four of them).
In the late 1950s the British-born critic and record producer
Stanley Dance supervised a fine series of LPs with the generic
title 'Mainstream Jazz' for Felsted: featuring musicians such as
Buck Clayton, Vic Dickenson, Coleman Hawkins, Johnny
Hodges, Charlie Shavers, Billy Strayhorn and Dicky Wells,
these provide some excellent musical definitions of the term.
The later, unrelated Mainstream record label was a venture of
ex-Mercury jazz record producer Bob Shad.

Mamie's Blues   'This is the first blues I no doubt heard in my
life,' said *Jelly Roll* Morton of 'Mamie's Blues', otherwise
known as '2.19 Blues': Mamie was Mamie Desdume, who
'could hardly play anything more, but she sure could play this
number' (Commodore, 1939). So could Jelly Roll Morton.

manzello   The *manzello*, defined by Brian Priestley as 'a curly
soprano sax' (*JOR* [2], 169), is – like the *strich* – among the
odder instruments played, often simultaneously, by Roland Kirk
(later Rahsaan Roland Kirk); the album *We Free Kings*
(Mercury, 1961) provides a fair cross-section of the results.

Maple Leaf Rag   By no means all of Scott Joplin's compositions made the transition from *ragtime* to core jazz repertoire:
'Maple Leaf Rag' is the one which most triumphantly succeeded
in doing so. It was named after the Maple Leaf Club in *Sedalia*,
Missouri, and composed in 1899.

mardi gras   The climax of the *New Orleans* carnival season,
culminating in the crowning of the Carnival King on Shrove
Tuesday. 'And during Mardi Gras – man! That's when we really
had fun,' said Kid Ory. 'All day and night bands marched up
and down the streets playing their heads off' (quoted in Shapiro,
31). When Louis Armstrong was crowned King in 1949 he
remarked: 'After that, I'll be ready to die' (quoted in Harris,
71).

matrix   Every shellac or vinyl record – that is, every record before
the CD – originates from a pair of matrices (or, if single-sided,

from a single *matrix*). With microgroove records, this fact may be of little interest, since identical information will be contained on a master tape; until the widespread adoption of magnetic tape in the late 1940s, however, each *take* of a number would be cut onto a separate *wax*, and consequently the identity of the matrix used for a particular commercial issue is of the utmost importance to collectors and discographers. The Charlie Parker sessions for Dial in September 1948 provide clear instances of this. 'Marmaduke' (B909) received no less than six complete takes, of which the last (B909–6) was chosen for the original issue; 'Parker's Mood' (B903) was finished in three, of which B903–1 and B903–3 (the original issue, and a masterpiece) are complete, while B903–2, abruptly ending in mid-chorus with a reed-squeak and resigned laughter from Parker, has a rather different sort of historical interest.

Because they are assigned at the time of recording, rather than at the time of issue or re-issue, matrix numbers are a far more reliable means than catalogue numbers of dating 78rpm records: this too can be helpful, since quite a few important jazz performances were recorded in poorly-documented or generally amnesiac conditions. For a telling example of the way in which matrix numbers can help to explain the character of a particular jazz record, see *Rocking Chair*.

mellow   To be *mellow* is to enjoy a state of relaxed, possibly drug- or alcohol-induced euphoria: 'Everything is mellow' means 'Everyone feels fine.' Ellington's 1940 composition 'In a Mellow Tone' – record sleeves and labels often print the title as 'In a Mellotone' – catches the mood nicely, and the subsequently added lyric by Milt Gabler (see *Commodore*) provides an amiable if undistinguished verbal equivalent.

Melody Maker   Founded in 1926 as a monthly magazine by music publisher Lawrence Wright, the *Melody Maker* under its first editor, Edgar Jackson, was deeply hostile towards black jazz musicians. Nevertheless, it was to develop into a weekly paper substantially devoted to jazz, although since the 1960s mostly concerned with pop music.

Memphis   Memphis, Tennessee, on the *Mississippi* River, was an early centre of jazz: 'We were playing in Memphis at the same time they were playing in Storyville in New Orleans,' said Buster Bailey (quoted in Shapiro, 85). At first the Memphis bands were 'just dance bands', reading from sheet music, but Bailey also remembered 'the first time W. C.Handy played "Memphis Blues", around 1916'; they began to improvise in 1917, after hearing *New Orleans* music on records.

Mezz Nickname of Milton Mesirow or Mezzrow (1899–1972), clarinetist, saxophonist and author of *Really the Blues* (1946).

Michigan Water According to 'Michigan Water Blues', attributed to Clarence Williams, Michigan Water 'tastes like sherry wine' whereas *Mississippi* Water 'tastes like turpentine'. But *Jelly Roll* Morton said that 'Tony Jackson used to play the blues in 1905, entitled "Michigan Water Tastes Like Sherry Wine"' (quoted in Shapiro, 248); Clarence Williams would have been twelve years old at the time.

Miles Along with Oliver, Armstrong, Gillespie and – arguably – more recent musicians such as Freddie Hubbard and Wynton Marsalis, Miles Davis (1926-91) belongs to that notable company which has made the *trumpet*, rivalled only by the *piano*, the most influential, innovatory and agenda-setting instrument in jazz. Though his use towards the end of his career of electric rock elements in his music must remain, for the time being at least, somewhat contentious, he has the distinction of having been involved in three of the indisputably great moments in recorded jazz history: the Charlie Parker quintet sessions for Dial and Savoy in 1947–8; the ground-breaking *Birth of the Cool* (Capitol, 1949–50); and *Kind of Blue* (Columbia, 1959), which 'is, quite simply, one of the most significant jazz records of the post-war years' (*JOR* [2], 62). Between the second and third of these came what Martin Williams has described as 'a musical rebirth ... the discovery of an intense, passionate, sometimes ravishing, highly personal trumpet style' (Williams, 201), encapsulated in two blues performances, 'Walkin'' and 'Blue 'n' Boogie' (Prestige, 1954).

minstrels According to Leonard Feather, *minstrel* show 'began about 1800 when a young singer from Germany, Gottlieb Graupner, did a blackface act at a Boston theatre, introducing himself as "The Gay Negro Boy"' (*BOJ*, 16). Minstrel shows were enormously popular throughout the nineteenth and into the twentieth century: the best-known group was undoubtedly Christy's Minstrels and the most successful composer of minstrel songs Stephen Foster. The parodic representation of blacks by whites now strikes us as grotesque, but it was certainly among the formative influences on jazz, and elements of the minstrel tradition were adopted – with varying degrees of irony – by black jazz musicians. Maurice Capel, in his essay 'The Metamorphosis of Orpheus', proposes a division of jazz musicians into saints, clowns, heroes, aristocrats, and free men; and of the 'clowns' – who include Armstrong and Waller – he writes: 'The "Uncle Tom" aspect or conventional minstrel image of their personality should not distract one from the subtle grandeur of their chosen part, and the "Clown" may be, in his own way, a Comedian putting his soul into his act and miming, like Harlequin, a freedom that he cannot live' (*Jazz Monthly*, January 1961, 4). See also *Old Folks at Home*.

Minton's   A venue in New York, Minton's Playhouse was the scene of the first experimental *bebop* sessions in the early 1940s, featuring such musicians as Kenny Clarke, Tadd Damerson, *Dizzy* Gillespie and Thelonious *Monk*.

Mississippi   The Mississippi River's unique position in the American myth – and, equally to the point, in the European myth of America – was permanently secured by Mark Twain in *The Adventures of Huckleberry Finn* (1884). Jonathan Raban, in *Old Glory*, recounts a widely-shared experience when he recalls how his childhood reading of *Huckleberry Finn* led him to search for the Mississippi in a huge old family atlas. He found it, 'wriggling down the middle of the page', and was immediately intoxicated by the names on the map: 'Just the sounds of Minneapolis ... Dubuque ... Hannibal ... St Louis ... Cairo ... Memphis ... Natchez ... Baton Rouge ... struck a legendary and heroic note to my ear' (*Old Glory*, 12); this echoes, no doubt unconsciously, Rex Harris's very similar list of 'romantic-sounding names' (Harris, 91) visited by Mississippi *riverboats* on their journeys from *New Orleans*. The notion that the river was responsible for the northward spread of jazz is at least partly a myth too, but the Mississippi remains a potent symbol of the way in which the music penetrated into the heart of the USA and of the cultural diversity which informed it.

Inhabiting this intensely evocative geography was one of jazz's pieces of formative good fortune. It seems pleasingly apt, too, in view of the music's substantially French origins, that a river and its settlements should resonate so strongly in it: the Mississippi-centred map of jazz is, in the extraordinarily powerful connotations of its names, only rivalled by maps of France's wine regions in *The World Atlas of Wine*.

MJQ The Modern Jazz Quartet, which evolved from the Milt Jackson Quartet in 1952, was a co-operative unit comprising Jackson (vibes), John Lewis (piano), Percy Heath (bass) and Kenny Clarke (replaced by Connie Kay, drums). Like that earlier wind-less ensemble, the Quintet of the Hot Club of France, the MJQ was a very long way from the *hot* jazz tradition: some listeners found its cerebral, eloquent music insipid; for others, it was the apotheosis of *cool*. Indeed, among the characters in Colin MacInnes's *Absolute Beginners* (1959) is 'a young coloured kid called Mr Cool': 'Cool is a local product, I mean born and bred on this island of both races, and he wears a beardlet, and listens to the MJQ, and speaks very low, and blinks his big eyes and occasionally lets a sad, fleeting smile cross his kissable lips ... what the hell he does to keep himself in MJQ LPs I haven't an idea – I really haven't (*Absolute Beginners*, 39). Philip Larkin, a more receptive jazz critic than he self-deprecatingly cared to admit, thought that 'their music, though narrow, has a natural swing under its shimmering restraint' (Larkin, 36), a judgement which neatly catches the paradox of the MJQ. The group recorded prolifically, for Prestige (1952–5) and Atlantic (1956 onwards).

moax Donald Clarke, explaining the title of Charlie Barnet's 1940 composition 'Afternoon of a Moax', says that '"moax" was a southern term for a square' (Clarke, 218); see *square*.

modern *Modern jazz* is essentially the generic term for the various stylistic innovations which occured from 1945 onwards, adopted as less restrictive and more respectable than *bebop*. Writing in 1950, Steve Race declared that the alternative had now become unusable 'in face of bebop dancers, bebop outfitters and bebop drug addicts' (quoted in Godbolt, 233). Until quite recently, most listeners recognised an arbitrary though quite serviceable tripartite division of jazz into traditional (or *trad*), *mainstream* and modern. Anyone who senses an anachronism in describing the music of the 1940s as 'modern' might reflect that the word continues to be applied to the poetry of thirty years earlier.

Monk Several great jazz pianists acquired nicknames – *Duke, Count, Fatha* – of an aristocratic or clerical nature; Thelonious Sphere Monk (1917–82) had no need of one. Either of his extraordinary forenames might have memorably stuck, but it was his surname which became synonymous with an equally extraordinary piano style: 'he seems not to have been influenced by anyone else,' says Tirro, 'and his style of playing seems to have attracted no students' (Tirro, 281). This is an overstatement: Monk's piano technique is, for all its abundant eccentricity, firmly rooted in *stride* - as when he quirkily resurrects a forgotten song called 'Darkness on the Delta' on an album recorded live at Philharmonic Hall, New York (Columbia, 1964) – yet it embraces such post-*bebop* dissonances as quarter-tones implied by simultaneously struck adjacent piano-keys; he had, in Leonard Feather's typically well-chosen words, 'an almost pathological aversion for playing the awaited chord at the expected moment' (*BOJ*, 67). Reviewing the film *Thelonious Monk: Straight No Chaser*, Nick Coleman wrote of him: 'In bamboo spectacles and halibut hat, he addresses the keyboard like a man pats an alligator' (*Time Out Film Guide*, 669). This sounds like a recasting of Whitney Balliett's similar-sounding though otherwise contrasting description of Monk as someone 'who approaches a keyboard as if it had teeth and he were a dentist' (*The Sound of Surprise*, 85).

Monk, three years older than Charlie Parker and an exact contemporary of *Dizzy* Gillespie, might have been recognised early on as an important member of the bebop generation; but his reputation remained muted, despite an important series of recordings for Blue Note in 1947, until he began to work with slightly younger musicians such as John Coltrane and Sonny Rollins in the mid-1950s. His reworkings of standard songs are intriguing: for instance, the wonderfully angular 'Smoke Gets in Your Eyes' (Prestige, 1954) on which, as Ira Gitler's sleevenote puts it, 'he weaves his solo statement of the melody through the loom of the sound'; the prismatic reinterpretations of an actually not-so-different pianist's work in *Monk Plays Ellington* (Riverside, 1955); or the syncopatedly askew version of 'Tea for Two' (Riverside, 1956). He was also the composer of numerous original pieces which have become established items in the jazz repertoire, including 'Epistrophy' (his signature-tune), 'Blue Monk', 'Misterioso', 'Evidence', '*Round Midnight*', 'Well You Needn't' and 'Ruby, My Dear' – the latter memorably performed on the album *Monk's Music* (Riverside, 1957) by that master of the *mainstream* ballad, tenor-saxophonist Coleman Hawkins, with Monk, Wilbur Ware (bass) and Art Blakey (drums). Monk's later recordings for Columbia, with a regular quartet featuring Charlie Rouse on tenor saxophone, mostly lack the freshness of his earlier work.

Monroe's Like *Minton's*, one of the places where *modern* jazz began to take shape, Clark Monroe's Uptown House was an important New York venue from 1936 until 1943, when Monroe moved to the *Spotlite* on *52nd Street*.

Mooche To *mooch* is to slouch or skulk (in England), to beg or cadge (in the USA); both meanings seem applicable to Ellington's lazily aggressive piece 'The Mooche' (Okeh, 1928), described by its composer as 'a stylised jungle' and 'a sex dance'.

Mood Indigo Ellington claimed to have taken only fifteen minutes to write this, his most famous composition: the definitive recording (Okeh, 1930) is – like that of its near-relation, 'Solitude' (Brunswick, 1934) – a masterpiece of evocative understatement. Another reason for the piece's enduring success is without doubt its wonderful title: see *blue*.

Moose the Mooche The innocent-looking title of this Charlie Parker number (Dial, 1946) is in fact the name of *Bird*'s Los Angeles heroin dealer.

Moten Swing 'The music of Bennie Moten's orchestra might be said to symbolize Kansas City jazz' (*JOR* [1], 233), and their 1932 Victor recording of 'Moten Swing' – note the confident use of that word so early in the *swing* era – is a significant transitional performance: it is based on the chord sequence of a popular song (Walter Donaldson's 'You're Driving Me Crazy') and it allows an unusually generous amount of space for solos, two characteristics abundantly found in the work of a younger *Kansas City* musician, Charlie Parker. The pianist on 'Moten Swing' is Bill, later *Count*, Basie.

moth-box A piano: in *Harlem*, 'even the poorest family had a "moth-box"' (Clarke, 161).

Motown Black pop music record label (and hence style) founded by Berry Gordy *c*.1960 in Detroit (= motor town = Motown). The music is distinct from and indeed antithetical to jazz in at least three respects: (i) the mechanically insistent beat lacks jazz's rhythmic flexibility; (ii) the instrumentation is essentially that of *rock 'n' roll*; (iii) though some Motown vocalists (for instance, Diana Ross) can treat a melodic line with subtlety, there is almost no scope, either vocally or instrumentally, for creative improvistaion. This is not to suggest that Motown performers necessarily lack talent: for example, Stevie Wonder (like earlier pianist-singers Nat Cole and Ray Charles) doubtless had the ability to be an excellent jazz musician but chose to use it in other ways.

mouldy fig   In the 1950s, 'a modernist's name for an ardent admirer of early jazz' (Ulanov, 96) or a *revivalist*; the expression is sometimes given additional, if perhaps superfluous, emphasis by the adoption of the mock-archaic spelling 'fygge'.

muggles   Marijuana cigarettes: 'Then the muggles took effect and my body got light' (Hoagy Carmichael, quoted in Shapiro, 144). 'Muggles' is the title of a number by Louis Armstrong and his Orchestra (Okeh, 1928), a typical instance of an innocent-looking nonsense word concealing a meaning known only to the *aficionado*.

Muskrat Ramble   One of the cornerstones of the *New Orleans* repertoire, 'Muskrat Ramble' was composed by *Kid* Ory, using material from nineteenth-century marches, in 1925; notable recordings include those by Ory himself with Armstrong's Hot Five (Okeh, 1926) and by Sidney Bechet with Henry Levine's *Dixieland* Septet (RCA Victor, 1950).

mute   A *mute* is a tone-modifying object placed in a *trumpet*'s or *trombone*'s bell. It has no place in the clean, somewhat strident brass sounds of *New Orleans* jazz but it became indispensable to the more complex textures of the orchestral jazz which evolved during the 1920s – notably in the form of the plunger and *wah-wah* mutes used in Ellington's bands. The plunger mute is a version of the familiar plumber's tool: 'In fact,' says Panassié, 'the first mute was a simple plumber's instrument used by Bubber Miley' (Panassié, 174).

N ew Orleans Unquestionably, New Orleans was the birthplace of jazz. The statement needs qualifying, of course: jazz was, after all, neither an invention nor a discovery but an evolving form of considerable diversity and complexity. Nevertheless, Rex Harris was correct in his assertion that 'if a new music or art form was to be born anywhere in the Southern States of America, then it had to be in New Orleans, by far the largest city south of St Louis and the entrepôt of trade for the whole of the Gulf region and the Mississippi hinterland' (Harris, 71). A sense of scale is needed: it had '216,000 inhabitants in 1880 – a population almost doubled since 1850' (Newton, 39); in present-day terms, bigger than Cambridge or Oxford, smaller than Bristol or Nottingham. Newton also points out that by 1910 the city contained 'at least *thirty* bands whose reputation has survived' (Newton, 37). 'The priority of New Orleans,' he adds, 'cannot be disputed.'

The reasons for this are complicated, and some of them will be found elsewhere in this book (for instance, under *jazz, Mississippi*). Apart from its geographical position – merely glancing at a map, at this *Crescent city* between a bend in the river and Lake Ponchartrain, gives you the sense of a place where things would happen – New Orleans had a particularly convoluted history: its French foundation and ownership briefly interrupted by a Spanish interlude had deep and lasting cultural consequences. The east side, downtown, 'contained the French opera, chamber ensembles, polished dance orchestra ... French New Orleans was peopled with white, black servants, and Creoles of Color – families of mixed blood'; west of *Canal Street*, uptown, was 'populated by newly freed blacks who were poor, uneducated, and lacking in all the cultural and economic advantages available to the Creoles of Color' (Tirro, 73). But this situation was altered beyond measure by the city council's racial segregation ordinance of 1894 and by the creation of the red-light district, *Storyville*, in 1897. The initially reluctant but ultimately inevitable interaction of European-influenced, notated *creole* music with indigenous, improvised black music is one of the many equations which produce jazz – as is the interaction of brass-led marching bands with the pianists of Storyville's bars, brothels and gaming-houses.

'The classic shape of a New Orleans band was trumpet (sometimes two), trombone, clarinet, banjo (or guitar), tuba and drums; later a piano and one or more saxophones were added and the string bass replaced the tuba' (Panassié, 178); that original line-up produced a pure, open, declamatory style of jazz which, according to New Orleans purists, was compromised by subsequent developments.

Newport The Newport (Rhode Island) Jazz Festival, founded by George Wein in 1954, rapidly became the most famous event of its kind in the world. It was there that in 1956 the faltering Duke Ellington Orchestra regained its momentum when Paul Gonsalves bridged the two parts of 'Diminuendo and Crecendo in Blue' with an astonishing solo of 27 choruses: 'The concert made headlines, the Columbia LP made the *Billboard* pop album chart and Duke made the cover of *Time* magazine' (Clarke, 338). Two years later, the 1958 festival was the setting for the most enduringly evocative jazz film ever made, Bert Stern's *Jazz on a Summer's Day* (1959).

NORK The New Orleans Rhythm Kings – an early but influential white band which featured clarinetist Leon Ropollo, cornetist Paul Mares and trombonist George Brunies – were originally formed as the Friar's Society Orchestra in 1921.

O DJB The *Original Dixieland Jazz Band* was a group of white New Orleans musicians formed in 1916 by drummer Johnny Stein as 'Stein's Original Dixieland Jazz Band'; they travelled to Chicago, where the other members dumped Stein and renamed the band under the leadership of Nick La Rocca. In 1917 they made some of the earliest jazz records (see also *Dixieland*), and in 1919–20 they successfully toured England. Their first London appearance, at the Hippodrome on 7 April, was indeed so alarmingly successful that the upstaged star of the evening, George Robey, threatened to quit unless the ODJB's engagement was terminated – which it was. Five days later they opened at the Palladium, after which 'they stayed in the country for fifteen months, doing good business at the Palladium, Rector's Club in Tottenham Court Road and the Hammersmith Palais' (Godbolt, 13); they even performed at Buckingham Palace before King George V.

Jazz on Record says of them: 'They played robust, funny-hat sort of jazz with immense spirit and a rather neurotic jumpy near-ragtime rhythm, and revelled in vulgar trombone slurs and comic effects with the clarinet' (*JOR* [1], 245). That is perhaps a little unkind, but only a little. Humphrey Lyttelton more generously concedes that 'they provided a sort of blueprint of how the line-up of trumpet-clarinet-trombone could be organised, and from that blueprint a lot of more creative jazz in what has come to be the Dixieland style has stemmed' (Lyttelton [1], 25).

ofay 'Sinatra was the first of the ofay sharpies' (Carr, 39): *ofay* is an adjective meaning white – 'fr. Yoruba *ofe* "a charm that lets one jump so high as to disappear", thus trouble' (Green, 195).

Okeh A record label of the General Phonograph Corporation, whose extensive pioneering work with jazz was initially due to the enthusiasm of recording manager Ralph Peer; bought by Columbia in 1926, Okeh then converted to the Western Electric recording system just in time to capture some of the finest performances of Armstrong, Ellington and others in remarkably accurate sound. 'I think one reason those records came out so well,' said *Kid* Ory, 'was that the Okeh people left us alone, and didn't try to expert us' (quoted in Shapiro, 115).

The jokily allusive initials 'OK', purporting to stand for 'Oliver King', were used as a reviewer's pseudonym by the jazz critic Brian Rust.

94

Old Folks at Home   Stephen Foster (1826–64), the leading American composer of the mid-nineteenth century, published his best-known song (subtitled 'Ethiopian Melody' and for contractual reasons credited to E. P. Christy of Christy's Minstrels) in 1851. It is significant in the pre-history of jazz both as an Americanisation of the English drawing-room ballad and as a sympathetic, if deeply sentimental, view of black America. The lyric as printed begins: 'Way down upon de Swanee ribber, Far far away, Dere's wha my heart is turning ebber, Dere's wha de old folks stay.' That now seems ludicrous and even offensive, but before dismissing it entirely we might mildly wonder whether its sentiments really differ greatly from those of the song which Louis Armstrong first recorded for Okeh in 1931, and which became his signature-tune for the next forty years, 'When It's Sleepy Time Down South'.

100 Oxford Street   One of the two longest-established jazz venues in London (the other is *Ronnie Scott's*): 'From 1942 it has, successively, been the home of the Feldman Swing Club, the London Jazz Club, the Humphrey Lyttelton Club and now the 100 Club' (Godbolt, 268).

Oop-Bop-A-Da   Although *scat* singing had been invented, or at any rate brought to public attention, by Louis Armstrong in 1926, it was not until the *bebop* movement of twenty years later that it fulfilled its surreally frenetic potential in numbers such as Dizzy Gillespie's 'Oopapada' (RCA Victor, 1947), a version of Babs Gonzales' 'Oop-Pop-A-Da' (Blue Note, 1947): 'Bebop anthems like "Oo-Bop-She-Bam", "Oo-Shoo-Be-Doo-Be", "Oop-Bop-A-Da" and "Ool-Ya-Koo" were scattergun vowel howls that burst out from somewhere between the beret and the goatee all along the 52nd Street clubs' (Carr, 22). One of commercial *rock 'n' roll*'s many direct debts to jazz is evident in the title of the Gene Vincent hit 'Be-Bop-A-Lula' (Capitol, 1956).

open horn   A trumpeter (or trombonist) who does not use a *mute* plays *open horn*, and the transition from one style to the other can be a momentous one: when Cootie Williams took over Bubber Miley's chair in the *Duke* Ellington band in 1929, 'Cootie had been playing open horn all the time, and when the guys heard about the change he was making, he got kidded a lot' (Duke Ellington, quoted in Shapiro, 213). As a very broad generalisation, it might be said that *hot* jazz trumpeters usually favour open horns whereas *cool* ones more often use mutes.

organ[1] The Hammond *organ*, says Leonard Feather, 'has been a welcome but reluctant guest at the jazz table since the 1930s' (*BOJ*, 140). It will be principally familiar through the work of *Fats* Waller in the 1940s and Jimmy Smith in the 1950s and 1960s: 'Without Jimmy Smith, jazz on the Hammond organ would not exist as we know it' (Ronald Atkins, *Guardian*, 23 March 1994). It can on occasion bring a wistful, elegiac quality to a slow ballad or *blues*, but it usually takes on a podgy and cumbersome air when anyone attempts to persuade it to *swing*. A *piano* generally does the job better.

organ[2] To *play organ* is to provide the supporting harmonic structure, in the form of organ-like chords, for a solo performer: 'Monk has fashioned a simple, poignant arrangemnt in which the band plays organ and he weaves his solo statement of the melody through the loom of the sound' (Ira Gitler, sleevenote to *Thelonious Monk Quintets* [Prestige, 1954]).

Oriole The first independent jazz record label in Britain, Oriole began releasing material from American *Vocalion* – including sides by Louis Armstrong, Duke Ellington, Jelly Roll Morton and Luis Russell – in 1927; it was owned by Levy's of Whitechapel, a record and gramophone shop which advertised 'The World's Finest Collection of "Red Hot" Dance Records' and was effectively the country's earliest dedicated jazz record retailer. After a long period of relative inactivity, Oriole had a creditable stab at rebuilding a jazz list (Realm) in the early 1960s before being sold by the Levy family to CBS in 1965.

Ornithology One of the numerous *Bird*-related titles which Charlie Parker gave to original compositions or reworkings of standards, 'Ornithology' (Dial, 1946) is based on the chord sequence of the Morgan Lewis/Nancy Hamilton song 'How High the Moon'; it is of particular interest because *Ella* Fitzgerald, in her version of 'How High the Moon' (Decca, 1954), re-introduced Parker's wholly new melodic line as a *scat* solo, a nice instance of how surprisingly compatible different branches of jazz can sometimes turn out to be.

orooni Part of a nonsense voabulary invented by Slim Gaillard:
Charlie Parker, for instance, was 'Charlie-Yardbird-Orooni' in
'Slim's Jam' (Bel Tone, 1945). In Jack Kerouac's *On the Road*,
Sal Paradise and Dean Moriarty go 'to see Slim Gaillard in a
little Frisco nightclub'. Gaillard, we're told, 'is a tall, thin Negro
with big sad eyes who's always saying "Right-orooni" and "How
'bout a little bourbon-oroonie"' (*On the Road*, 166). See also
vout.

Papa The trumpeter Oscar 'Papa' Celestin (1884-1954) was one of the great *New Orleans* pioneers, leader of the Original *Tuxedo* Orchestra from 1910 and the Tuxedo Brass Band from 1911; he recorded with his Original Tuxedo Jazz Orchestra for *Okeh* in 1925. His later recordings are disappointing, but he became a revered elder statesman of New Orleans, as John A. Provenzano noted in *Hear Me Talkin' to Ya*: 'Oscar "Papa" Celestin, now well on his way to his seventies, has the jazz world on its toes ... [he] has set an example that the present young generation of bottle-man tooters would do well to follow' (quoted in Shapiro, 80). 4,000 people marched at his funeral procession.

Parker, Charlie See *Bird*

Parker's Mood This magnificent blues, recorded by Charlie Parker for Savoy in 1948, provides the most eloquent evidence of the underlying continuity between early jazz and the postwar *bebop* musicians: 'The final version of "Parker's Mood",' says Max Harrison (prompted to almost comparable eloquence himself), 'is, indeed, one of the greatest blues improvisations ever to be recorded, and it vibrates in the mind for long afterwards, like a cry echoing through the dark and endless forests of a dream' (Harrison, 18).

patuni 'The term "sweet patuni" has been much used as a vaginal image by blues performers, because, according to Paul Oliver, it comes from the form of the petunia flower' (*PBJ*, 93). Gregory R. Staats, in the essay just quoted, notes several variants such as 'Sweet Patunia', 'Sweet Patuna Stomp' and 'I'm Wild About My Patootie'.

pee wee 'A nickname for any noticeably small person' is Jonathon Green's kindly definition (Green, 208): jazz's notable examples include *Chicago* clarinetist Pee Wee Russell, *Dixieland* trumpeter Pee Wee Erwin, and the inimitable master of ceremonies at *Birdland*, Pee Wee Marquette.

Perdido 'Perdido' is a Latin-tinged composition by Ellington trombonist Juan Tizol, while Perdido Street in *New Orleans* is memorialised in Louis Armstrong's 'Perdido Street Blues'.

piano Although it often assumes an apparently unglamorous supporting role, the *piano* is the single instrument without which jazz could not have existed. The musicians of *ragtime* were predominantly pianists; while in *Storyville* it was the pianists who acted as catalysts in the transformation of street music into jazz. *Front-line* players and singers more readily achieve fame as soloists, but pianists – such as Jelly Roll Morton, James P. Johnson, Duke Ellington, Earl Hines, Art Tatum, Bud Powell and Thelonious Monk – have predominantly shaped the music as composers, arrangers and technical innovators. Nor should one forget musicians such as Duke Jordan or John Lewis whose most enduring contributions may be as finely sympathetic accompanists, the Gerald Moores of jazz. 'There is an unbroken Olympian lineage at the top of jazz,' writes Whitney Balliett (his nominees are Morton, Ellington, Basie, Monk and Lewis), 'which has been distinguished by the curious fact that all its members are composers, arrangers, leaders, and pianists' (*Dinosaurs in the Morning*, 67-8).

Jazz piano-playing has moved through various styles and fashions – some of which, such as *ragtime, stride,* or *boogie-woogie,* have more or less useful names – but its most striking evolutionary characteristic has been called 'the case of the disappearing left hand'. As Miles Kington has pointed out, the repetitive left-hand figuration of the great stride players 'was essentially a style for solo pianists. Stride piano not only needed no other instruments, but other instruments would have got in the way' (*Jazz Journal*, September 1965, 28). Even where early jazz pianists were successfully integrated into bands as providers of harmonic and rhythmic stability, their emphatic and unvarying left-hand patterns steadily became redundant, if not actually obstructive, as the music became increasingly subtle and complex.

In his story 'Sonny's Blues', James Baldwin rightly insists that the piano, no less than a blown instrument, has to be somehow inhabited by its performer: 'He has to fill it, this instrument, with the breath of life, his own... And a piano is just a piano. It's made out of so much wood and wires and little hammers and big ones, and ivory' (*Going to Meet the Man*, 140).

pickup band An ad hoc group of musicians brought together for a specific concert or recording date, a far more common practice in jazz than is usually suspected by the layman. While some bands, such as Ellington's, retained relatively stable personnel, many star soloists fronted any group of musicians as 'their' band or orchestra, including the most eminent of them all, Louis Armstrong: the Hot Fives and Sevens existed only in the studio; 'Louis Armstrong and his Orchestra' of 1929 was in fact Luis Russell's band; and many dates and recordings thus labelled consist of Armstrong plus the house band of whatever venue he was appearing in. During the 1930s, *pickup bands* made an enormous number of recordings, some of them excellent, for the expanding *jukebox* market. From the 1940s onwards the vacuous phrase 'All-Stars' was frequently attached to the name of a leader or a venue, really meaning 'musicians who happened to be available, some of whom you might even have heard of'.

plunger The kind of *mute* made famous by trumpeter Bubber Miley with the *Duke* Ellington orchestra in the 1920s – especially in 'Black and Tan Fantasy' (Brunswick, 1927); he was replaced in 1929 by the *open horn* player Cootie Williams, but 'before you knew it everyone was saying nobody could work with a plunger like Cootie' (Duke Ellington, quoted in Shapiro, 213). The other great plunger exponent of the day – in the rival Fletcher Henderson band – was Joe Smith, of whom Kaiser Marshall recalled: 'I have never seen anyone get the tone and sweetness out of a trumpet with the plunger like Joe could' (quoted in Shapiro, 209).

pops Various musicians, most notably the bass player (George) Pops Foster, have acquired this nickname, which usually implies affectionate seniority. There may well be the suggestion that those earning titles like Pops or *Daddy* are a bit too long in the tooth to call themselves *cats*, as in this exchange from 'Now You Has Jazz' (*High Society*, Capitol, 1956). Bing Crosby: 'Hey, Pops, you want to grab a little of what's left here?' Louis Armstrong: 'Yeah, Daddy, yeah.' Armstrong, though universally known as *Satchmo*, was almost invariably addressed as Pops. Ulanov notes that Benny Goodman was in the habit of calling 'everybody, from a stranger in the house to his own daughter, "Pops"' (Ulanov, 92).

Potato Head Blues The title of this number, recorded by Louis Armstrong and his Hot Seven for Okeh in 1927, is described by Humphrey Lyttelton as 'an uncomplimentary but jovial reference to some person unknown' (Lyttelton, 135); since 'potato jack' is 'illicit liquor, distilled in US prisons' (Green, 218), the implication may well be alcoholic. Francis Newton suggests that either 'West End Blues' or 'Potato Head Blues' 'would probably win in a poll for the best single jazz record ever made' (Newton, 112); of the two, for this listener, 'Potato Head Blues', with its perfect construction and magisterial second solo by Armstrong, is the clear choice. Lyttelton's detailed analysis of the track is a matching masterpiece of insight and enthusiasm, and his conclusion that 'after this, jazz would never be the same again' (Lyttelton [1], 137) wholly justified.

praline A French quadrille which evolved into one of the most celebrated of all *New Orleans* numbers: 'Originally called "Praline" – a ragged kind of candy – it was known in Storyville as "Get Out of Here and Go Home"' (Stearns, 60). After two further metamorphoses, it was recorded by The Original Dixieland Jazz Band in 1917 as 'Tiger Rag'.

Pres Short for 'President', *Pres* – sometimes Prez – was the nickname of tenor-saxophonist Lester Young (1909–59); he was called it by Billie Holiday whom he, in a gesture of mutual admiration, nominated as First Lady or *Lady Day*; both worked with *Count* Basie in the late 1930s and recorded together, with the Basie band and with other musicians, for Columbia. Before that, Young had played with Fletcher Henderson's orchestra, where he succeeded Coleman Hawkins in 1934: the contrast between Hawkins and Young – the two most influential tenor stylists in jazz – was thus established early on. Hawkins, though an invigorating swinger when occasion demanded, was a player of breadth and warmth; Young, by contrast, often seemed cerebral and 'cool', long before that word took on its specific jazz meaning: 'His tone was pale where Hawkins's had been rich, he phrased leanly where Hawkins seemed florid' (*JOR* [1], 330). Whitney Balliett cites 'the axiom that Young and Coleman Hawkins are the totally divergent leaders of the cool and hot methods of playing their instrument', but goes on rightly to point out that both musicians were 'always after the same thing – a controlled lyricism' (*Dinosaurs in the Morning*, 35).

Nowhere is that 'controlled lyricism' more finely achieved than in 'Blue Lester', a quintet track recorded with the Basie rhythm section (Savoy, 1944), a few weeks after two other memorable larger-group sessions, also for Savoy. A traumatic period in the US Army during 1944 and 1945 had musical as well as personal consequences, vividly illustrated in a sequence of recordings with both *mainstream* and *bebop* musicians: the tone is harder, the treatment of melody more fragmented, and the results range from near-incoherence to overwhelming intensity; the version of 'These Foolish Things' (Aladdin, 1945) is a masterpiece of re-invention comparable to Parker's

'Embraceable You' and a fascinating contrast to Young's more conventionally lyrical pre-Army treatment of the same tune (Savoy, 1944). During the 1950s, like so many of his contemporaries, Young appeared with a diverse range of musicians for Norman Granz's Jazz at the Philharmonic concerts and recorded for Granz's Clef and Verve labels. In this, as in his perceived artistic decline, his later career again ran in parallel with Billie Holiday's, and he died after collapsing during an engagement in Paris in March 1959, three months before Lady Day herself.

Preservation Hall An unusual *New Orleans* venue, intended to provide a platform for neglected if often legendary older musicians in somewhat austere surroundings, Presevation Hall was founded in 1961: 'The audience sits and listens, and sometimes contributes to the kitty. There is a $5 fine for requesting "The Saints"' (Larkin, 116).

Rabbit   'Nickname of Johnny Hodges, because of his profile' (Panassié, 203), or alternatively, according to Geoffrey Smith, 'because of his taste for lettuce' (*Jazz Record Requests*, BBC Radio 3, 21 December 1996); hence, as is typically the case with jazz nicknames, titles of tunes such as 'Meet Mr Rabbit' and 'Rabbit Pie', and of albums such as *Blue Rabbit* (Verve, 1964) – the latter prompting a somewhat desperate sleeve illustration of a carrot dipped in a pot of blue ink.

race   Where British record companies from the 1920s onwards coined phrases such as 'rhythm style series' in order to avoid the word 'jazz', their American counterparts preferred *race* or *sepia* series. Since then, of course, the question of race and jazz has become an ideologically fraught one: while it may now appear racist to suggest that black musicians have a particular facility for jazz, it must also seem ungenerous (and historically indefensible) to deny that this has mostly been the case. Clearly, black musicians were very largely responsible for the evolution of jazz and they provide its unquestionably towering figures – Armstrong, Ellington, Parker. I think it is also clear, simply from the evidence of one's ears, that *in general* white musicians took a long time to get it right: early *Dixieland* almost always sounds like the imitative art it is; even the greatest white musicians of the *swing* era, such as Benny Goodman, can sound effortful beside their black contemporaries. Now this may, of course, have nothing to do with race and everything to do with social and environmental factors. But, for whatever reason, it seems to me that the decisive shift to a white jazz which sounds properly experienced and created rather than skilfully imitated comes in the next musical generation with *cool* players such as *Chet* Baker, Stan Getz and Gerry Mulligan. It hardly needs to be said that race is no guarantee of the matter one way or the other: for instance, the technically accomplished and inventive black pianist Oscar Peterson seems to many ears to lack the intuitive rhythmic subtlety of his white contemporary Bill Evans. That, however, is the exception rather than the rule: there is every reason to insist that jazz is not just America's but *black* America's gift to twentieth-century music, and for those of us who are neither black nor American to accept it with grace and gratitude.

ragtime   This piano style, which 'flourished for about twenty years – from 1896 to 1917' (Stearns, 104), was a major ingredient in early jazz. *Ragtime*, says Francis Newton, 'was almost exclusively a style of solo pianists, trained in European music and often with high musical ambitions' (Newton, 36); and Joachim Berendt also emphasises its European characteristics: 'Everything important can be found in it: from Schubert, Chopin and, most of all, Liszt, to marches and polkas – but all recast in the Negro's rhythmic conception and dynamic way of playing' (Berendt, 6). This debt would be repaid, notably in Stravinsky's *Ragtime* (1918).

OED finds its earliest citation for 'ragtime' in W. H. Krell's 'Mississippi Rag' (1897), but Rex Harris notes 'the first recorded use of the word itself in 1893, when a Detroit composer by the name of Fred Stone had a song published which he called "Ma Ragtime Baby"' (Harris, 57); since neither Krell nor Stone were otherwise figures of particular importance, it seems very likely that they found the word already in use elsewhere. Leonard Feather suggests that 'the first and greatest of the ragtime pianists' may have been Louis Chauvin, 'a pale-skinned, slight youngster whose features were more Indian and Spanish than Negro' and who died at the age of 28, leaving only 'three published compositions and the memory of contemporaries who recalled the exquisite originality and beauty of his work' (*BOJ*, 17). Harris cites Tom Turpin of St Louis (who published his 'Harlem Rag' in 1897) as ragtime's first major figure, while the most prolific composer of rags was undoubtedly Scott Joplin: 'between 1898, when his "Original Rags" came out, and 1917, which saw the issue of "Reflections", he was responsible for some fifty rags and popular tunes flavoured with the "rag" idiom' (Harris, 59). It seems appropriate that the worldwide revival of interest in Joplin's work should have been principally due to the work of an early-music scholar and Bach specialist, Joshua Rifkin.

Ragtime, 'with its florid, fulsome right hand and "umpy-dump bottom"' (Lyttelton [1], 161) was an important early influence on pianists such as *Jelly Roll* Morton, James P. Johnson and *Duke* Ellington – that neat phrase 'umpy-dump bottom' is Ellington's – but its comparative rhythmic rigidity was a limitation which jazz quickly outgrew. 'In itself,' as Martin Williams says, 'ragtime proved to be a kind of blind alley, but its contribution to jazz, and to form in jazz, is probably immeasurable' (Williams, 19). According to Russ Cassidy, the 'last of the ragtime composers' was Joseph Lamb (1877–1960), whose 'last published rag, "Bohemia", appeared in 1919' (*Jazz Monthly*, August 1961, 7).

ramble The *New Orleans* street bands played in funeral processions: 'Sometimes,' Wingy Manone recalled, 'it took them four hours to get the cemetery.' Once there, the assembled company 'chanted questions, such as "Did he ramble?" "Did he gamble?" or "Did he lead a good life until the police shot him down on St James Street?"' (quoted in Shapiro, 30). To *ramble* is to become loquacious with drink, or simply to drink: as the mock-morbid prologue to *Jelly Roll* Morton's 'Didn't He Ramble?' (RCA Victor, 1939) has it, 'Ashes to ashes, dust to dust: if the women don't get you, the liquor must.' *Kid* Ory's composition 'Muskrat Ramble' (1925) drew on nineteenth-century New Orleans march motifs.

Rampart Street One of the legendary streets of *New Orleans*, running from the Navigation Canal to *Storyville*.

Red Henry 'Red' Allen (1908–67) was one of jazz's great transitional figures, a trumpeter who worked with both Luis Russell and Fletcher Henderson – two of the finest bandleaders of the 1920s and 1930s – as well as Coleman Hawkins and Billie Holiday: 'he was one of the most creative figures of his era,' says Albert McCarthy, 'and, in all probability, the last great trumpet soloist to come from New Orleans' (*JOR* [2], 4).

red beans and rice As inseparable a part of Louis Armstrong's personality as his signature tune, 'When It's Sleepy Time Down South', in whose prologue they figure; Armstrong was also fond of signing letters, such as those to Leonard Feather (quoted in *From Satchmo to Miles*, 21-4), 'Am Redbeans and Ricely Yours' – on at least one occasion varied to the quite splendid 'Am Brussell Sproutsly Yours'.

Red Hot Peppers This band of *Jelly Roll* Morton's made a series of records for Victor between 1926 and 1928 which are 'among the greatest of all jazz recordings' (*JOR* [2], 206), rivalled in their period only by those of the Armstrong Hot Five and Seven.

Red Onion A *barrelhouse* or *honky-tonk* in *New Orleans* where Louis Armstrong and Johnny Dodds played; Armstrong led a band called the Red Onion Jazz Babies in 1924.

reeds The increasing use of reed instruments – usually called simply *reeds* – was perhaps the greatest single factor in the changing texture of jazz during the 1920s and 1930s: the only reed in a typical New Orleans *front line* was the *clarinet*; but within a decade the invasion of the saxophones had taken place, and arrangers for *big bands* were even able to think in terms of 'reed sections'.

refrain   The phrase *with vocal refrain*, common on 78 rpm record labels, indicates a vocal passage of unspecified length in an otherwise instrumental performance: see *chorus*.

release   Same as *bridge passage* or *middle eight*.

rent party   During the 1920s and 1930s the *rent party*, to which an admission fee would be charged, developed into a widespread and highly organised means of circumventing Prohibition laws, providing income for the jazz musicians who performed there and, of course, paying the householder's rent.

revivalist   Two complementary *revivalist* movements – in the USA in the late 1940s and in Britain in the early 1950s – attempted to rescue jazz from such perceived distortions as *swing* and *bebop* and to restore the true *New Orleans* tradition. The problems with this were twofold: firstly, revivalist bands were often saddled with a suffocating earnestness, an evangelical urge to melt down every saxophone and expunge every deviant modernist harmony; secondly, as soon as they shed this unseemly puritanism, they all too readily descended into the populist pastiche of the Firehouse Five or Acker Bilk's Paramount Jazz Band. Committed modernists called revivalists *mouldy figs*.

rhythm   In the long years before the word *jazz* attained a measure of respectability, 'rhythm' was often employed as a benign euphemism: for instance, the celebrated series of jazz record drawn from *Okeh* and issued by Parlophone from 1929 onwards were billed as the 'New Rhythm Style Series'.

rhythm section   Essentially that group of jazz instruments which are struck or plucked rather than blown, as opposed to the *front line*. In a medium-sized or large band, the rhythm section will comprise all or most of the following: *piano, guitar* (or possibly *banjo*), *bass, drums*. Not all these may be present in smaller groups, while a pianist-leader may feel the need to insist on his status: hence, such billings are 'Fats Waller and His

Rhythm' or 'Erroll Garner and His Rhythm'.

'A history of the jazz rhythm section,' says Martin Williams, 'is virtually a history of the music.' He points out that whereas in the early 1920s one might have found 'a pianist's left hand, a string bass or tuba, a guitar or banjo, a drummer's two hands, and perhaps his two feet, all clomping away, keeping 4/4 time, or two beats out of the four', this primitive time-keeping gradually disappeared, partly because it was no longer needed by the front line but also 'because the rhythm section men found something to put in its place' (Williams, 118).

ride cymbal A single cymbal, either mounted on the bass drum or free-standing, struck with stick or brush.

riff 'A short, simple, repeated phrase' (Panassié, 210), of two or four bars: the repetition provides emphasis and intensity. In 'the original version of "Mahogany Hall Stomp" [Okeh, 1929], one of Louis Armstrong's choruses consists of a simple riff repeated six times' (Panassié, 211). The *riff style* was especially associated with Kansas City: Charlie Parker's 'Now's the Time' is 'a blues with obvious roots in the Kansas City riff music of Parker's youth' (Harrison, 19). For some later musicians, the riff is a symbol of restriction: 'We're living in a riff society... it's just not so easy being an individual in this society' (Ornette Coleman, quoted by Linton Chiswick, *Independent*, 22 September 1995).

ringshout 'The ringshout is an African dance that features a group of singers circling counterclockwise around the leader of the religious chant' (Tirro, 58); it was a formative influence on New York *stride* piano and, according to Rudi Blesh, was danced in some *Harlem* churches as recently as 1950.

rip An upward glissando, often found in virtuoso New Orleans *trumpet* solos; a more stately version, on *clarinet,* is at the opening of Gershwin's *Rhapsody in Blue.*

riverboats The Mississippi paddle-steamers provided not only transport but also entertainment: 'The larger steamers carried a jazz band, and there was a wide space under cover on the top deck for dancing' (Panassié, 212). At 'places with romantic-sounding names, Baton Rouge, Natchez, Vicksburg, Arkansas City, Memphis, Cairo, Paducah, right on to St Louis and beyond, the boat would pull in for excursion trips, staying an evening, a day, or even many weeks at a big city like St Louis' (Harris, 91).

In 1907, the riverboat-owner Joseph Strekfus hired Fate Marable as bandleader and, subsequently, talent-spotter. Tony Catalano recalled how in 1919 Marable dropped in at a dance where *Kid* Ory's band was playing: 'Fate asked who was playing the trumpet, and it turned out to be Louis Armstrong ... Fate went up to Lyons [the band's manager] and asked if he could use the trumpet man the nights Lyons didn't use him ... and that's how Louis got his start to get out and go north, as Fate gave him steady work on the *Capitol* of the Strekfus Lines' (quoted in Shapiro, 83-4). This account provides a useful counterbalance to one of the myths of jazz history by implying that the rewards and pleasures of playing the riverboats had at least as much to do with the northward drift of musicians as the closure of *Storyville*. Nor, indeed, was that drift exclusively northward, as John Steiner usefully points out: 'On the contrary, Fate Marable... took several musicians *down* the river on the boats, recruiting several better-educated hornmen to improve the versatility of his winter bands based in New Orleans' (Hentoff, 149).

Riverside   New York jazz record label, named after 'Riverside Blues', founded by Bill Grauer and Orrin Keepnews in 1953: its output was divided between a historical reissue programme (originally released in the UK as the London *Origins of Jazz* series in the 1950s) and a 'Contemporary Series' comprising repertoire comparable to that of its rival *Blue Note*; it was bought by the Berkeley-based Fantasy group in 1972.

rock 'n' roll   '"Riding", "rocking", and "rolling" are words applied both to the railroad and to coitus' (Newton, 6): with jazz's usual happy knack of assimilating sexual slang, they appear in numerous blues and song lyrics, often sounding childishly innocuous to innocent ears. 'Tin Pan Alley's assumed naïveté in matters of sex reached a high point of hilarity with the advent of "rock 'n' roll",' as Humphrey Lyttelton has pointed out. 'Translated from Negro slang into the jargon of the police-court reporter, "Rock Around the Clock" literally means "have sexual intercourse every hour, on the hour"' (*Spectator*, 31 July 1964).

Rockin' Chair   This number was composed by Hoagy Carmichael and first recorded by him with Louis Armstrong fronting Luis Russell's orchestra on 13 December 1929 (Okeh, published matrix 403496C), immediately after Armstrong's momentous 'St Louis Blues' (403495B): the relaxed, loping performance of 'Rockin' Chair' finds the band wonderfully unwinding after the frenetic track which preceded it.

Ronnie Scott's   London's best-known jazz club opened in Gerard Street in 1959 and moved to Frith Street in 1965; with the exception of *big bands*, which simply wouldn't fit into the available space, every visiting American jazz musician of any consequence has played there. Ronnie Scott's own performing career as a *tenor* saxophonist represents the archetypal British jazz life: as a teenager he joined first Ted Heath's band, then 'Geraldo's Navy', working on Cunard liners; after the war he played with Ambrose's Orchestra, the bands of Vic Lewis and Jack Parnell, and hung out with the *Archer Street* jazzmen; during the 1950s – a period when *modern* jazz in England evolved into a highly convincing variant of the American *West Coast* style – he performed and recorded with his own and other groups including the Jazz Couriers, which he co-led with Tubby Hayes. Ronnie Scott died in 1996, shortly before his seventieth birthday. Like John Dankworth and Humphrey Lyttelton, he was one of the major shaping spirits of post-war jazz in Britain.

Roseland   A New York ballroom at which Fletcher Henderson's orchestra – including Louis Armstrong, Coleman Hawkins and Don Redman – regularly appeared in the early 1920s: it was 'a "whites only" hall pandering to white tastes' (Godbolt, 60).

Round Midnight   The Thelonious *Monk*/Cootie Williams number 'Round Midnight' (copyrighted in 1954 but possibly composed as early as 1939) is the most haunting of all jazz *ballads*: the definitive recording – inward, halting and meditative – is almost inevitably the solo one by Monk himself (Riverside, 1957). *Round Midnight* is also the title of an affectionate 1986 film about jazz directed by Bertrand Tavernier.

Royal Gardens   The Royal Gardens (subsequently the Lincoln Gardens) in *Chicago* was a dance-hall where *New Orleans* musicians such as *King* Oliver and Sidney Bechet played in 1918–19; according to Tommy Brookins, 'The Royal Gardens could contain a thousand people' (quoted in Shapiro, 103). 'Royal Garden Blues' (1919) is yet another place-memorialising composition by Spencer Williams (cf. 'Basin Street Blues', 'Mahogany Hall Stomp') in collaboration with the unrelated Clarence Williams.

Royal Roost   The name of this New York night-club reflects, according to Clayton and Gammond, 'its origins as a chicken-in-the-basket restaurant' (*Jazz A–Z*, 207); the fact that it is closely associated with Charlie Parker, or *Bird*, who played there in the late 1940s (as did *Miles* Davis and *Dizzy* Gillespie), is therefore apt but coincidental.

Ryan's   One of the most important venues on New York's *52nd Street* in the late 1930s and early 1940s. It was in 1939 that Milt Gabler, of the *Commodore* music shop and record label, 'started running the Sunday sessions at Jimmy Ryan's as another way of giving jazzmen work... There was a moment there, in 1941–2, at the Ryan sessions, when hot jazz seemed at its purest' (Max Kaminsky, *My Life in Jazz*, 121–2). Among the enormous number of musicians whom Kaminsky lists as appearing at Ryan's were Sid Catlett, Bill Coleman, Red Allen, J. C. Higginbotham, Pee Wee Russell, Vic Dickenson, Bud Freeman, Zutty Singleton, Billy Butterfield, Roy Eldridge, Wilbur and Sidney DeParis, Barney Bigard, Buck Clayton, Lester Young, Earl Hines and Meade Lux Lewis.

St James Infirmary   A dirge-like traditional number, of which the definitive recording, including the slightly macabre lyric, was made by Louis Armstrong and his Savoy Ballroom Five (Okeh, 1928).

St Louis   St Louis, Missouri, 'is frequently referred to as the birthplace of ragtime' (Stearns, 107); it was also the birthplace of T. S. Eliot, which gives added point to 'that Shakespherian Rag' in *The Waste Land*.

St Louis Blues   Composed in 1914 by W. C. Handy, 'St Louis Blues' is 'the most popular of all blues, and one of the most frequently played jazz numbers' (Panassié, 217). In fact, it is something altogether more odd and complicated than the *blues* it claims to be, and it perfectly illustrates the hybrid nature of jazz even at this relatively early stage. Reflecting a fashionable interest in Afro-Spanish rhythms, Handy 'used a *tangana* rhythm in the verse' (Stearns, 59), while 'the last chorus of "St Louis Blues" owes its melody to the exhortations of Brother Lazarus Gardner, Presiding Elder of the A.M.E. Church of Florence, Alabama, according to W. C. Handy' (Stearns, 77). The singer Alberta Hunter recalled that 'it was at the Panama [in Chicago] that I introduced the "St Louis Blues" ... I was there a long time and people like Bert Williams and Al Jolson would come to hear me sing "St Louis Blues"...' (Shapiro, 94). Bessie Smith's recording of the song with Louis Armstrong (Okeh, 1925) is 'the epitome of the classic-blues performance, and the equality of the vocal and cornet solo work is extraordinary' (Tirro, 134); a film called *St Louis Blues*, starring Bessie Smith, was made by Warner Brothers in 1929.

Saints   *Saints* is the familiar if not always altogether friendly shorthand for 'When the Saints Go Marching In', an anonymous piece dating from jazz's pre-history. It was tolerably recorded by Louis Armstrong (Decca, 1938) and subsequently featured by every amateur *Dixieland* band on the planet: on these occasions, its instant recognition rather than its musical interest conventionally wins loud applause. Such is the piece's tiresome notoriety that there was a $5 fine for requesting it at *Preservation Hall*.

Salt Peanuts   One of the quintessential *bebop* numbers, composed by *Dizzy* Gillespie and Kenny Clarke in 1943 and recorded by Gillespie for Musicraft in 1944. Art Pepper recalls

111

the shock of hearing it on his return from war service in Europe:
'I had never heard anything like that. I said, "My God, nothing
can be like that"' (quoted in Gitler, 153).

salty According to Ulanov 'angry, irritated' (Ulanov, 96): Papa
Charlie Jackson's 'Salty Dog Blues', which he recorded with
Freddie Keppard (Paramount, 1926), is not about a condiment.

Saratoga A club in *Harlem*, where Luis Russell's outstanding
band – which included trumpeter Henry *'Red'* Allen and trombonist J.G.Higginbotham – played in 1929-30.

Satchmo 'Nickname of Louis Armstrong, short for "Satchel-
mouth"' (Panassié, 217). Armstrong (1900–71) shared with
Duke Ellington the chronological good fortune of being the ideal
age for jazz: both men were in their mid-twenties in the mid-
1920s, and both were to enjoy long careers of almost unflagging
distinction. Armstrong served his apprenticeship with the
greatest of the first-generation jazz bandleaders, Joe *'King'*
Oliver, on whose 'Chimes Blues' (Gennett, 1923) he played his
first recorded solo; Lil Hardin, the pianist on that session, was
shortly to become Mrs Louis Armstrong. In 1924 he joined –
and as a solo voice rapidly came to dominate – Fletcher
Henderson's orchestra. The extensive series of records made for
Okeh by Armstrong's Hot Five, Hot Seven and Savoy Ballroom
Five between 1925 and 1929 – many of them, including 'Potato
Head Blues' (1927) and 'West End Blues' (1928), in remarkably good electric recordings – together comprise one of jazz's
greatest monuments: they are 'the finest jazz records ever
recorded' (Panassié, 7), 'the Complete Shakespeare of jazz'
(Larkin, 46). Other major achievements of these years include
the Armstrong-Earl Hines duet 'Weather Bird' (Okeh, 1928),
as audaciously 'modern' a piece as much *bebop* of twenty years
later, and – among many tracks with larger bands – the version
of 'St Louis Blues' (Okeh, 1929) which Philip Larkin called 'the
hottest record ever made' (Larkin, 230) and the original
recording of Armstrong's signature tune 'When It's Sleepy Time
Down South' (Okeh, 1931). As early as 1926 he was being billed
by Joe Glaser as 'The World's Greatest Trumpet Player'.

Armstrong's lengthy association with American Decca
(Brunswick in the UK) from the mid-1930s onwards produced
the mixed blessings usually associated with that label (cf. *Ella,
Lady Day*): fine recordings interspersed with novelty numbers
and collaborations with other artists on the same roster, such

as the Mills Brothers. In fact, this was a perfectly sensible way to sustain a musical career, far preferable to re-treading the pioneering days of the 1920s. This did become a danger, however, with Armstrong's post-war 'All-Stars', a sometimes inspired but more often routine-sounding band which coincided with the New Orleans revival led by George Lewis and others. By now, Armstrong had become a star of a different sort, as famous for his ebullient personality and distinctive singing as for his trumpet-playing, appearing in films and at festivals all over the world: when one of his albums was called *Ambassador Satch* (Columbia, 1956), the title was no more than the truth. In the mid-1950s Norman Granz produced a successful series of LPs teaming him with Ella Fitzgerald (Verve, 1956-7), while in the 1960s Armstrong recorded such popular hits as 'Hello Dolly' and 'What a Wonderful World' – enterprises somehow redeemed by Satchmo's incomparable good humour and his unfaltering delight in entertaining.

Savoy[1] The name of two important jazz venues: the *Chicago* ballroom, opened in 1927, which gave its name to Louis Armstrong's Savoy Ballroom Five and Kid Ory's 'Savoy Blues'; and the *Harlem* dance-hall, 'the home of happy feet', where Chick Webb's orchestra regularly appeared in the 1930s, which gave *its* name to 'Stompin' at the Savoy', written for Webb by Edgar Sampson in 1933. The latter, Mary Lou Williams recalled, 'was a place of tremendous ethusiasm and the home of fantastic dancing... Webb was acknowledged king and any visiting band could depend upon catching hell from little Chick' (quoted in Carr, 32). When the visiting band was Benny Goodman's, 4,000 people crowded in and another 5,000 were turned away.

Savoy[2] Herman Lubinsky's New Jersey-based record label, founded in 1942, whose impressive jazz output included definitive performances by both Charlie Parker and Lester Young. When Savoy re-released tracks from the 1944 Tiny Grimes 'Tiny's Tempo' session under Parker's name, cashing in on the latter's subsequent fame, 'Parker's own comment in 1950 about this news was that "Herman Lubinsky does a gang of things he's not supposed to do", while his companion Chan Richardson added, "They say he has eleven sets of books"' (Priestley, 88).

scat This distinctive vocal technique, comprising 'rhythmic nonsense syllables... that helped listeners to feel the stylistic connection between [Louis Armstrong's] singing and his playing' (Priestley, 26) was, according to jazz legend, accidentally invented by Armstrong. While recording 'Heebie Jeebies' (Okeh, 1926), he apparently dropped the sheet music and consequently improvised the first *scat* solo: this whimsical gibberish proved so popular that it became a permanent feature of Armstrong's performances and was adopted by a number of later jazz singers. Of 'Heebie Jeebies' Humphrey Lyttelton, dismissing the dropped-sheet-music theory, perceptively adds: 'The result, paradoxically, is to make the song seem much less nonsensical than it does in its natural state' (Lyttelton [2], 16). This is quite often the case with scat interruptions to otherwise inane lyrics.

Scat singing was reinvented by the post-war *bebop* generation, when the nonsense lyrics of Slim Gaillard collided with the melodic invention of musicians like Parker and Gillespie. 'The Royal Family of scat were Sarah Vaughan, Ella Fitzgerald, Betty Carter, Leo Watson and Mel Tormé' (Carr, 24); slightly later but equally notable contributions to the art – which is, according to Tormé, 'the toughest kinda singing' – came from Anita O'Day and Carmen McRae.

screamer   Among the crowd-pulling spectacular effects favoured by big bands of the *swing* era were high-pitched, ear-splitting *trumpet* solos, whose perpetrators were aptly called *screamers*; some of them, such as *Cat* Anderson and Maynard Ferguson, were also fine musicians.

Sedalia The town in Missouri which 'first witnessed the growing fame of Scott Joplin' (Stearns, 107); hence, a name for the original style of *ragtime*.

send From the early days of jazz until the late 1950s (when, as is the way with slang, the expression quite suddenly became unthinkably absurd), *to send* was to induce in the listener a state of euphoric involvement in which any conceivable distraction was blocked out by the music. The fact that alcohol or drugs were often in close proximity to the jazz producing this effect may not be coincidental. 'I put a disc on to his hi-fi, my choice being Billie H., who sends me even more than Ella does ...' (Colin MacInnes, *Absolute Beginners*, 19).

sepia Used as a euphemism for 'black' or 'negro', principally in the 1930s and 1940s when several record companies had *race* or *sepia* lists; Duke Ellington characteristically turned the word to evocative good use in his composition 'Sepia Panorama' (RCA Victor, 1940).

session musician A freelancer employed on specific recording dates to work, for instance, on film soundtracks or pop records: many jazz musicians, including some of the finest, have supplemented their irregular incomes in this way.

set A live band will often play for twenty or thirty minutes before taking a break: a session of this length is called a *set*, and the word may also be used for the group of numbers making up an LP or CD – a 'set of tracks'.

seventy seven In 1947, Doug Dobell converted his father's bookshop at 77, Charing Cross Road, WC2 into the most famous jazz record shop in Britain and arguably in the world; it was a mecca for jazz fans for over thirty years until the site was (amid much protest) redeveloped. During the 1950s and 1960s Dobell sporadically issued jazz records on the Seventy Seven label.

sharp Apart from its usual, more general musical sense, *sharp* in the language of jazz means 'fashionable, felicitous' (Ulanov, 96). This is one of that cluster of words on the *cool* or *hip* side of jazz which lays claim to a fashionable self-awareness utterly distant from the rather ramshackle image of the *revivalists*. The link between cool playing and sharp dressing was especially close in the 1950s, not only in America but in Britain too, as is clear from the work of Colin MacInnes. His 1959 essay 'Sharp Schmutter' perfectly demonstrates how the vocabularies of jazz and fashion had become fused: after describing 'the aggressively elegant silhouette of any sharp English working-class boy today' he went on to wonder 'what will this sharp cat's bird, or chick, have on' (*England, Half English*, 149, 153).

shave According to Gregory R. Staats, the term *shave 'em dry* ('an expression indicating intercourse without preliminary love-making') was 'as favoured among female singers as the sweet petunia had been favoured by male singers' (*PBJ*, 94); no less a figure than *Ma* Rainey herself recorded a song called 'Shave 'Em Dry' for Paramount in 1924.

shit[1] Marijuana: '... being in Texas, I could get all the "shit" I wanted, and I used to send him [Billy Taylor] "shit", and he'd send me records' (Zoot Sims, quoted in Gitler, 152).

shit[2] Rubbish: 'Woody was just starting to change and get away from the old shit ...' (Jimmy Rowles, quoted in Gitler, 154).

shuffle Defined as 'a variant of boogie woogie rhythm' by Panassié, who notes its use by some *New Orleans* and many *Chicago* musicians (Panassié, 224), *shuffle* rhythm was anathema to the emerging *bebop* players of the mid 1940s. Billy Eckstine – then an important bandleader for whom both Parker and Gillespie worked – remembers Art Blakey joining the band in St Louis, 'and Art started playing shuffle and Diz stopped right in the middle of what he's been [playing] and, man, we jumped right in and said, "Man, don't play that shit, don't ever play no shuffle"' (quoted in Gitler, 130).

sideman A *sideman* is any musician in a band apart, obviously, from the leader.

sit in A musician, perhaps a distinguished visitor, who plays along with a band for pleasure and without payment is said to *sit in*. Often this is as spontaneous and relaxed as it sounds, but it may also be a way of evading legal restrictions. A justly celebrated example of the latter occurred at the Winter Garden Theatre in London on 13 November 1949: the billed performance was by Humphrey Lyttelton's Band, but the capacity audience, well-briefed by the jazz grapevine, knew that Sidney Bechet would be in the audience. His visit to England was a strictly non-performing one: at customs, he had explained that his *soprano* sax was a valuable instrument which never left his side when an immigration official said, 'You're not going to play it, I hope' (Godbolt, 244). Nevertheless, he was unsurprisingly prevailed upon to sit in with the Lyttelton band, whereupon, as *Jazz Illustrated* reported, he 'commenced to treat the excited audience to the most wonderful session of jazz ever heard in this country' (Godbolt, 240).

skiffle Originally a name applied in the 1920s to some American folk-blues music, *skiffle* became popular in Britain thirty years later, following the success of 'Rock Island Line', performed by a group led by Lonnie Donegan from within Chris Barber's Jazz Band and taken from their LP *New Orleans Joys* (Decca, 1954).

The skiffle group was essentially designed to add variety to the band's programmes (and to give the *front-line* players a break), but Donegan's popular success soon eclipsed his leader's and he went on to record a sequence of hit singles, only one of which, 'The Battle of New Orleans' (Nixa, 1958), had even the most tenuous nominal connection with jazz.

slap 'A sound produced by plucking the strings of a string bass in such a way that the string slaps against the neck of the instrument' (Panassié, 226); Panassié rightly points out that the technique was mainly used by *New Orleans* musicians before 1935, though it should be noted that Ellington's first string bassist, Wellman Braud, occasionally used it in the context of a larger band.

slap tongueing A saxophone player's trick of 'producing a freakish, hollow tone by slapping the reed against the mouthpiece rather than vibrating it' (Lyttelton [2], 75). Coleman Hawkins used it in his earlier years, until he dramatically modernised his technique after hearing the pianist Art Tatum: 'he immediately started creating another style for himself, based on what he heard Tatum play that night – And forever after dropped his slap tongue style' (Rex Stewart, quoted in Gitler, 48).

slurring Another technique primarily applicable to the *alto* and (especially) *tenor* saxophone – and in large measure responsible for the latter's immense popularity as a *ballad* instrument slurring 'has nothing to do with slithery up-and-down movements from one note to another', even though that is how it may sound: 'Notes that are slurred simply move from one to the other without separate "tongueing" or articulation' (Lyttelton [2], 74–5).

Smack 'Smack' is heroin, which probably has nothing at all to do with Leonard Feather's composition 'Smack!', recorded by Coleman Hawkins and the Chocolate Dandies (Commodore, 1940): the title is actually a reference to the nickname of bandleader and arranger Fletcher Henderson, for whom Hawkins had worked in the early 1930s. Louis Armstrong remembered the telegram he received late in 1923 asking him to join the 'great Fletcher Henderson's orchestra. That's how I felt about "Smack" Henderson' (quoted in Shapiro, 202). Henderson's was the first of the jazz big bands, equalling and – in the years up to 1927, while Don Redman was arranging for it – even surpassing that of *Duke* Ellington in numbers like 'Henderson Stomp' and 'Hot Mustard' (Brunswick, 1926); but his shaky business sense, which became shakier after he received head injuries in a car crash in 1928, destablised the band. During the 1930s, the band's personnel – including musicians such as trumpeters Henry Allen and Rex Stewart, trombonists J. C. Higginbotham and Benny Morton, and saxophonists Benny Carter and Coleman Hawkins – was always distinguished but always changing. Subsequently, Fletcher 'Smack' Henderson worked as an arranger, notably for Benny Goodman in the late 1930s and into the 1940s.

Small's   In *Harlem* in the mid-1920s, 'Small's was the place to go, the one spot where everybody'd drop in' (Duke Ellington, quoted in Shapiro, 171). Among the musicians Ellington recalled at Small's Cabaret (subsequently the Paradise) were Jack Teagarden, Benny Goodman and – soon to join his own orchestra – Johnny Hodges.

sock cymbal   Another name for the *high hat* – a pedal-operated pair of cymbals.

solid   Current in both *swing* and *bebop* circles, *solid* has the slightly odd meaning of 'excellent' or 'brilliant' in contexts where 'fluid' might have seemed more appropriate: 'That's solid,' says Slim Gaillard approvingly in 'Slim's Jam' (Bel Tone, 1945).

soul   The element of spiritual and emotional authority which authenticates a genuine jazz performance, *soul* is most easily recognised by its absence – in, for example, the bloodless virtuosity of many an operatic singer who 'crosses over' into jazz repertoire with grotesque results. And yet – to take an opposite view for once – it is plainly absurd for the jazz purist to suggest that a fine performance of a Bach passion or a late Beethoven quartet or a Mahler symphony is devoid of soul: *all* great music performed with skill and commitment has it. In some simplistic, overtly populist jazz of the 1960s and in much commercial black pop music, 'soul' means something rather different: here the balance between musical invention and emotional statement is inordinately skewed towards the latter, and the results are often, paradoxically, bland and uninteresting.

South Side   Like *Storyville* in New Orleans and *Harlem* in New York, the South Side in *Chicago* was the jazz area of the city: Coleman Hawkins, who spent his schooldays in Chicago, 'used to go down to the South Side to hear the jazz musicians' (quoted in Shapiro, 207).

Spanish tinge   The 'Spanish tinge' was *Jelly Roll* Morton's name for the Latin influence in *New Orleans* jazz: see also *tangana*.

Spasm Band   An early variant of the *jug* band, in which young and/or impoverished players used home-made instruments: Panassié gives the personnel of the earliest known spasm band, playing in *New Orleans* in 1895, as 'Harry Gregson, leader, singing through a length of gas-pipe; Stalebread Charlie (Emile Lacomb) on cigar-box fiddle; Cajun (William Bussey) harmonica; Charlie Stein on kettle, cow-bells and gourd; Chinee on bull-fiddle; Warm Gravy, Whiskey (Emil Benrod) and Monk (Frank Bussey) on various home-made whistles and horns' (Panassié, 236). These musicians were all between twelve and fifteen years old.

Speckled Red   One of the true *barrelhouse* pianists, Speckled Red was a 'half blind and albino Negro' (*JOR* [2], 272) called Rufus Perryman; his brother, Willie Perryman, also a pianist, was known as Piano Red.

spiritual   The gospel song or negro *spiritual* is – like its secular equivalent, the *work song* – one of the strands of black American folk music which had a formative influence on jazz: it never became fully integrated with the rapidly-changing instrumental core of jazz, however, and it survived instead as a parallel and complementary form whose star performer and commanding presence was undoubtedly Mahalia Jackson (1911-72).

Spontaneous Music Ensemble   The former Dankworth trumpeter Kenny Wheeler founded Britain's first *free jazz* group, the Spontaneous Music Ensemble, in 1966. It was well-regarded by some listeners, and even Philip Larkin felt he 'should mention' their LP *Challenge* (Eyemark, 1967), 'the first British free form disc, according to the sleeve, though I went to sleep during it' (Larkin, 198).

spook breakfast   A 4 a.m. session, especially at the Kentucky Club in *Kansas City*, so named 'because "spooks" or "ghosts" stayed up all night' (Gitler, 155).

Spotlite In the mid 1940s, the Spotlite became the most influential of the many jazz clubs on New York's *52nd Street,* featuring major *bebop* musicians including Gillespie and Parker. The name was later revived by a British record label specialising in the reissue of important bebop performances.

square Any seriously un*cool* person – a *longhair,* perhaps – who has no understanding or appreciation of jazz: 'square' was so widely used in the 1950s that the expression itself became corny and uncool, and hence self-negating.

standard song Though there are numerous and fascinating exceptions to this general principle, the *standard* American popular song consists of a 32-*bar* unit subdivided into eight-bar sections arranged in the pattern AABA: the B section is known as the *middle eight* or *bridge passage.* The key relationship between the main theme and the middle eight is usually tonic to subdominant, the latter introduced by a diminished seventh, or *blue note,* in the tonic chord. Thus, a song in C might be expected to have a middle eight in F, the modulation accomplished via a chord of C7 (C E G B♭), while one in F might be expected to have a middle eight in B♭, modulating via a chord of F7 (F A C E♭): in practice, though not necessarily in notation, the bridge passage adds a flat to the key signature. Quite apart from the flattened nature of blue notes themselves, this provides one practical reason for the tendency of jazz to favour the 'flat' keys of F, B♭, E♭ and A♭ – the other being the fact that many of the conventional *front line* instruments are tuned in flat keys (clarinet and trumpet in B♭, alto sax in E♭, for instance).

Two simple examples in the key of F, expressed as chords, will suggest some of the harmonic possibilities of this formula. The first is Hoagy Carmichael's 'Georgia on my Mind', omitting the seldom-performed introductory verse; note how the famously plangent effect of this song depends on the substitution of D minor for the expected B♭ in the middle eight, introduced by the unlikely yet wholly plausible chord of A7:

F - - - | A7 - - - | Dm - - - | Gm - B♭m - |
F - E7 - | Gm - G9♭5 C7 | F - F♯dim - | Gm6 - - C7+ |

F - - - | A7 - - - | Dm - - - | Gm - B♭m - |
F - E7 - | Gm - G9♭5 C13 | F - - - | - - A7 - |

Dm - Gm - | Dm - B♭7 - | Dm - Gm - | Dm - G7 - |

Dm - Gm - | Dm7 - E7 - | Am Am7 F♯dim B♭9 | Am - C7 - |

F - - - | A7 - - - | Dm - - - | Gm - B♭m - |
F - E7 - | Gm - G9♭5 C13 | F - - - | - - - - |

The second is 'Just a Sittin' and A-Rockin'' by Billy Strayhorn
and Duke Ellington. Again, the introductory verse is excluded.
The fascination here is the way in which, typically, a theme of
perilous harmonic banality blossoms into an utterly triumphant
middle eight in A, reached by the chromatic slide from Gm7
through F6 to E7:

B - F7 - | B♭ - F F+7 | B♭ - F - | B♭ - F F+7 |
B♭ - F - | B♭ Ddim - - | F - Dm7 - | B♭6 Gm7 F6 F7 |

B♭ - F - | B♭ - F F+7 | B♭ - F - | B♭ - F F+7 |
B♭ - F - | B♭ Bdim - - | F - Dm7 - | B♭m6 Gm7 F6 E7 |

Am - C+ - | Am7 - Am6 - | Am - - - | - - Dm6 E7 |
A - - - | - - - - | Bm7 - E9 - | Gm7 - C9 - |

F - F7 - | B♭ - F F+7 | B♭ - F - | B♭ - F F+7 |
B♭ - F - | B♭ - Bdim - | F - Dm - | Gm7 C9 F6 - |

Some of the most gifted composers and songwriters of the
century – such as George and Ira Gershwin, Cole Porter, Jerome
Kern, Richard Rogers and Lorenz Hart, Harold Arlen, Johnny
Mercer – cast their finest work in the form of standard songs,
transforming the popular music of their time and providing an
incomparable range of material for jazz musicians.

stick   A slang name, abbreviated from *gobstick* or *liquorice stick*,
for the *clarinet*.

stomp   With charming if rather useless candour, Panassié
describes 'stomp' as 'A word with no technical significance',
adding for good measure that it doesn't even 'denote a number
played in fast time' (Panassié, 240). No, but it certainly isn't
normally used to describe a number played in *slow* time: etymo-
logically identical with 'stamp', it implies a piece which is
rhythmically fairly forceful and repetitive, and was used quite
indiscriminately by early jazz musicians in titles (such as 'King
Porter Stomp') as a brisker alternative to *blues*.

stop time   A technique which creates solo space by reducing
the accompaniment to a single chord on the first beat of alter-

nate bars; Tirro notes that it 'derives from a common accompaniment pattern used to support tap dancing' (Tirro, 434).

Storyville   The official red-light district of *New Orleans*, including *Basin Street* – '... what white historians call "Storyville", but everyone at the time knew as "the district"' (Russell Davies, *Listener*, 6 August 1981) – opened in 1897 and by 1910 comprised cabarets, 'dance schools', *honky-tonks*, *barrel-houses*, gambling joints and 'almost two hundred houses of pleasure' (Ramsey and Smith, *Jazzmen*, 12); it was named after Alderman Sidney Story who, intending to limit the spread of vice in New Orleans, effectively created a ghetto dedicated to prostitution and jazz. 'Lewd women were not permitted to occupy any house, room, or closet outside of Storyville,' writes Frank Tirro. 'At the height of its activity, there were probably between 1,500 and 2,200 registered prostitutes in Storyville, and the sporting houses employed everything from string trios to ragtime pianists and brass bands' (Tirro, 73).

The creole clarinettist Alphonse Picou cheerfully recalled those 'happy days, man, happy days ... There were two thousand registered girls and must have been ten thousand unregistered. And all crazy about clarinet blowers' (Shapiro, 21). One of the best of those 'white historians' mentioned by Russell Davies offers a different perspective: 'A visitor to the red-light district of Storyville might have heard the brittle tinkle of a sporting-house piano coming from behind the lace curtains of a Basin Street "mansion", or the turbulence of a New Orleans band cutting through the smoke and the reek of cheap perfume in a Franklin Street cabaret, the clarinet weaving a throbbing counterpoint, above the cornet's sober lead, the trombone underlining their statement and thrusting the band forward with renewed impetus' (Charles Fox, in McCarthy, 26). This is evocative, and the precedence given to that 'sporting-house piano' is significant; for, as Marshall Stearns points out, 'Storyville helped to establish a special kind of jazzman: the solo pianist' (Stearns, 58), and jazz as we know it was born when the more accomplished of these pianists joined forces with the better musicians from the marching-bands. *Jelly Roll* Morton was the most celebrated of the Storyville pianists: after heading north in 1912, he 'helped to spread the newer style in the course of his endless travels' (Stearns, 59). The marines finally closed down Storyville in 1917, a scene noisily recreated in 'Farewell to Storyville', from the 1946 film *New Orleans*, which featured such musicians such as Louis Armstrong, Kid Ory and

Barney Bigard, and ludicrously cast Billie Holiday as a maid.
After 1917, 'the ladies scattered to ply their trade elsewhere,
and many of the musicians moved north to Chicago' (Panassié,
241).

In the 1960s 'Storyville' became the name of a record label
devoted to authentic New Orleans jazz; Alderman Story, one
suspects, would not have been much amused by being thus
memorialised.

strich The *strich* is an eccentric reed instrument resembling a
straightened *alto* sax, part of the musical armoury of Roland
(later Rahsaan Roland) Kirk; see also *manzello*.

stride The style of Harlem-based pianists such as Eubie Blake
and James P. Johnson: 'The four left-hand beats per bar ... now
become a dynamic rhythm-section, not least because of the
expenditure of energy in moving the hand two octaves or more
between each beat and the next – hence the name of "stride"'
(Priestley, 7). The legacy of *stride* is audibly present in the work
of major jazz pianists such as *Duke* Ellington, Earl Hines and
Thelonious *Monk*. The late Don Pullen 'was a player of
immense passion, able to look forward in free music and back-
wards to stride playing in the same few moments' (Steve Voce,
Independent, 30 May 1995).

strings Although individual stringed instruments have an
honourable place in jazz – either in the *rhythm section* or in
the hands of soloists such as Django Reinhardt (guitar),
Stephane Grappelly (violin) or Charles Mingus (bass) – listeners
have often had reservations about large string sections which
tend to be unwieldy and unswinging, even though it was bandleaders of the *swing* era like Artie Shaw and Harry James who
were principally responsible for bringing them into jazz. Some
indisputably great soloists have been very fond of them,
however, and the cushiony blandness of a large string section
can occasionally provide the perfect foil for an exquisite jazz
ballad performance, as in Charlie Parker's 'I Didn't Know What
Time It Was' (Clef, 1949) or Billie Holiday's 'Don't Worry
About Me' (Verve, 1959). One of the most eccentric uses of
strings in jazz is to be heard in the work of Bill Le Sage's
'Directions in Jazz Unit', comprising a sextet of leading British
musicians plus a quartet of cellos, on *The Road to Ellingtonia*
(Philips, 1965).

Sunset[1]   A *Chicago* jazz club owned and run by Louis
Armstrong's manager Joe Glaser: it was here that Armstrong
fronted Carroll Dickerson's orchestra, with whom he recorded
for Okeh in 1928–9.

Sunset[2]   A *Kansas City* jazz club owned and run by Piney
Brown: it was a 'wild Twelfth Street spot' with 'a bartender
named Joe Turner, and while Joe was serving drinks he would
suddenly pick up a cue for a blues and sing it right where he
stood, with Pete [Johnson] playing piano for him' (Mary Lou
Williams, quoted in Shapiro, 285).

sweet   Although *sweet* can have a pejorative sense, implying that
a performance is sentimental or slickly commercial, its more
specific jazz meaning – as in 'sweet and hot' – is favourable,
describing a light and deftly swinging touch.

swing[1]   As Berendt points out, *swing* has two senses in jazz: the
first 'connotes a rhythmic element' and 'is present in all styles,
phases, and periods of jazz' (Berendt, 15). Or, as Duke Ellington
put it: 'It don't mean a thing if it ain't got that swing.'

swing[2]   'During the decade of 1935 to 1945, a period known as
the "Swing Era", the greatest mass conversion in the history of
jazz took place' (Stearns, 140). Swing turned a populist but
minority musical form into a popular one with mass appeal,
blurring the boundary between jazz and dance music, making
international stars of bandleaders such as Harry James, Artie
Shaw and, above all, Benny Goodman. Goodman was the 'King
of Swing' who 'convinced the audience, set the standards for
performance, became the spokesman for the new music, and in
every way was the most important and successful popular,
dance, and jazz musician in America from the mid-depression
years to the end of World War II' (Tirro, 232). Tirro identifies
four characteristics which differentiate swing from earlier jazz:
'First, the size of the bands; second, the arrangements; third,
the characteristics of the solos; and, fourth, the change in the
habits of the rhythm section' (Tirro, 235). Of course, swing did
not emerge instantaneously – fully-arranged *big band* jazz had
been evolving from the earliest days of the *Duke* Ellington and
Fletcher Henderson orchestras – but the new style was nevertheless distinctive, not least in its crowd-pleasing musical
pyrotechnics and consequent commercial success.
    The astonishing suddenness of this success was facilitated by
two non-musical factors: the launch of the Ritz cracker and the

time-zones of the USA. To promote their new product in 1935, the National Biscuit Company sponsored a radio programme called *Let's Dance*, on which the Benny Goodman band appeared alongside those of Xavier Cugat and Kel Murray, and this was broadcast coast to coast by 53 stations. When Goodman embarked on his nationwide tour in May, the reaction on the East Coast, where *Let's Dance* was heard after 11 p.m., was cool; but when the dispirited band eventually reached the Palomar Ballroom in Los Angeles, where the programme went out at mid-evening peak-time, they were amazed by their reception: 'I don't know what it was,' said Goodman, 'but the crowd went wild and then – boom!' (quoted in Shapiro, 306). 'The Swing Era,' as Marshall Stearns justly claims, 'was born on the night of 21 August 1935' (Stearns, 150).

Sternly purist jazz critics, such as the young Charles Fox, were not impressed: 'Swing began to pay good dividends ... artistry became the quality least needed by the purveyors of this synthetic culture,' he wrote in 1946. 'Goodman, Shaw, Dorsey – this was the triumvirate idolised by the swing-crazy, uncritical youth, eager only for the physical thrill that a swing-band brought them. Speedily the band leaders found that a tasteful hot solo played in the middle register of the instrument made no apparent impression, but a squealing hit-or-miss venture into top register never failed to draw applause, while the spectacle of a drummer, his jacket patched with sweat [Fox surely has in mind a famous photograph of Gene Krupa], jibbering and grimacing in a multisonous orgasm, excited their shrillest admiration' ('The Development of Orchestral Jazz', in McCarthy, 37). Though this somewhat extreme view is not one which Fox would have fully endorsed later on, it is nevertheless a widely held one: Francis Newton, only a little more moderately, describes swing as 'a combination of increasingly insistent rhythm and considerable noise' (Newton, 55). Certainly, it is possible to see the big bands of the swing era as in some respects an aberration between two phases – *New Orleans* and *Bebop* – of more obviously authentic small-group jazz.

Symphony Sid   Sid Torin, a New York disc jockey on radio and at the *Royal Roost,* was an early and influential advocate of *bebop*. He is immortalised in Lester Young's 'Jumpin' with Symphony Sid' (Aladdin, 1947).

syncopation   The great red herring of the jazz vocabulary, *syncopation* was often invoked by unsympathetic critics as a defining feature of jazz, the implication being that it was some altogether non-European form of African rhythmic mumbo- jumbo. But it is Percy Scholes who surprisingly provides a perfectly straight-forward definition – 'Syncopation is a displacement of either the beat or the normal accent of a piece of music' – and who subsequently adds: 'All composers of all periods have used syncopation' (Scholes, 1006-7). His music example is from Mozart. That said, displaced accents and stressed off-beats are indeed characteristic features of jazz and of one of its main components, *ragtime*.

Tailgate In *New Orleans*, when the members of a band were crowded onto a *bandwagon*, the trombonist would be at the back, his instrument projecting over the *tailgate*: 'that part of the wagon over which the trombonist draped himself and his horn, so that the slide wouldn't poke out the eyes of friends and colleagues' (Charles Edward Smith, in Hentoff, 35). A *trombone* played in an exuberantly New Orleans style is consequently called a 'tailgate trombone'.

take One recorded performance of a number: a particular session will often include several *takes* of a piece, of which the most satisfactory (or least unsatisfactory) will be chosen for isuue. This was necessarily the case with 78 rpm records, before the use of magnetic tape. Since the late 1940s, it has been possible to combine, with increasing accuracy and sophistication, material from several performances: most jazz musicians and listeners rightly frown on this, however, preferring the coherent integrity of a single take whenever possible. A commercially usable performance is a 'good take', a flawed or incomplete one a 'bad take'. Dave Brubeck's well known 'Take Five' (Columbia, 1961) is a double pun on this sense, alluding both to the expression meaning 'Take a five-minute break' and to the fact that the composition is in 5/4 time.

talk Particularly expressive players of brass and reed instruments are said to *talk* – to treat their horns and woodwinds as if they were extensions of the human voice: 'More than any of the others who play melody instruments, Jim [Robinson] "talks" with his trombone. Sometimes he growls – sometimes he yells – then he makes a short speech, or converses with George Lewis's clarinet' (Frederic Ramsey Jnr, in McCarthy, 19). Buster Bailey said of *King* Oliver: 'With an ordinary tin mute, he could make the horn talk' (quoted in Shapiro, 102). But just as any instrument, even an unblown one, can be called a *horn*, so any instrument can talk: 'The dry, low, black man said something awful on the drums, Creole [a bass player] answered, and the drums talked back' (James Baldwin, *Going to Meet the Man*, 140). Hence the jazz exclamation and title 'Hear me talkin' to ya!', aptly borrowed for the famous oral history of jazz by Nat Shapiro and Nat Hentoff.

tangana A Spanish rhythm incorporated by W. C. Handy in '*St Louis Blues*' (1914) and elsewhere; the widespread use of 'Afro-Spanish rhythms such as the tango and the rhumba, which

127

Jelly Roll Morton called the "Spanish tinge"' (Stearns, 59) is one example of the cosmopolitan, inclusive character of early jazz.

tear out   To *tear out* is to play uninhibitedly or, in an exactly parallel phrase, to let rip: 'The boys didn't really hear me *tear out* until one night we all were mugging on "Tiger Rag", and believe me, it was on' (quoted in Shapiro, 203).

tempo[1]   As in other musical forms, the pace at which a piece is performed, which can be expressed as a metronome reading but is more often indicated verbally: typical instructions on jazz sheet music include 'moderately fast', 'medium slow beat', 'slow ballad tempo'. To be 'in tempo' is to keep good time, possibly after a passage of looser *ad lib* introduction or improvisation. 'The word is also used to designate certain rhythmic nuances: New Orleans tempo, Savoy tempo, Lunceford tempo' (Panassié, 250).

Tempo[2]   A small but important specialist North London-based jazz record label, initially devoted to reissues of rare early performances and subsequently to modern British jazz; acquired by Decca and operated as a division of *Vogue* until the early 1960s.

territory bands   In the 1930s, these were 'groups (black or white) who had a strong following in their own region of the US and had local hit records, which then led to them being promoted on a nationwide basis' (Priestley, 60). Some, like the Erskine Hawkins band from Alabama, cited as an example by Priestley, eventually achieved considerable success with 'Tuxedo Junction' and 'After Hours' (Bluebird, 1939); most remained relatively obscure. *Territory bands* provide a fascinating area for exploration beyond the major figures of jazz: as with the lesser-known areas of any art, much of their work is pedestrian or crude but the quite frequent surprises are thus all the more rewarding. The second edition of *Jazz on Record* mentions the following among others: the George E. Lee band (Kansas City); Walter Page's Blue Devils (Oklahoma City); the Original St Louis Crackerjacks (St Louis); Zack Whyte's band (Cincinatti); Alphone Trent's band (Arkansas); the Original Yellow Jackets (Arkansas); Troy Floyd's band (San Antonio); Boots and his Buddies (San Antonio); the Ross-De-Luxe Syncopators (Florida); Taylor's Dixie Serenaders (North Carolina); the Carolina Cotton Pickers (Charleston) (*JOR* [2], 382–5).

However, Ira Gitler rather disparagingly recalls that when he
was in the midwest in the 1940s, territory bands 'meant
white, "mickey mouse" bands out of Mankato or Sioux Falls'
(Gitler, 13).

third stream 'I coined the term as an *adjective*, not as a noun,'
said Gunther Schuller in 1962. 'I conceive of it as the result of
two tributaries – one from the stream of classical music and one
from the other stream, jazz – that have recently flowed out
towards each other' (quoted in Balliett, *Dinosaurs in the Morning*,
214). Schuller insisted that, while the two major streams would
remain essentially undisturbed, a degree of creative fusion was
inescapable among musicians and listeners exposed to both
traditions, and he added: 'Kids in universities where I speak
think nothing of playing a Charlie Parker record right after *Eine
Kleine Nachtmusik.*' Though the influence of *third stream* music
was perhaps less profound than Schuller might have hoped (it
was treated with predictable wariness on both sides), his sense
of weakening barriers was a prescient one, for during the past
thirty years examples of musical 'cross-over' have become
commonplace. It may be noted too that the origins of jazz
itself in the late nineteenth century resulted from just such
a synthesis of disparate European and American musical
traditions.

tickler An itinerant *ragtime* pianist, whose repertoire might
range from popular songs to – in the case of James P. Johnson
– 'rag variations on the William Tell Overture, the Peer Gynt
Suite and even the relatively modern Prelude in C Sharp Minor
by Rachmaninoff' (Lyttelton [1], 28). This unusual virtuosity
provoked hostile critics to indignant fury: '"Jazzing the Classics"
became an accepted term for a detestable practice,' grumbled
the *Oxford Companion to Music* (Scholes, 535), a peculiar
complaint since variations on works by other composers have
always been an accepted part of European music. When *Jelly
Roll* Morton first visited New York, he was apparently (and
uncharacteristically) overawed by the musicianship of the *ticklers* there: these may have included Eubie Blake (subsequently
known as the composer of *standard songs* such as 'Memories
of You'), Raymond *'Lippy'* Boyette, Stephen Henderson,
Luckey Roberts, Corky Williams, John *'Jack the Bear'* Wilson,
and of course James P. Johnson himself. 'A "real smart tickler",'
Lyttelton notes, 'would wear a military or coachman's overcoat
… complemented by a distinguished hat' (Lyttelton [1], 29),

thus proving that sartorially eccentric pianists existed long before Thelonious *Monk*.

tight The phrase 'tight like that' may 'refer to the physical union of lovers or may be used as a description of hard times or difficulties', according to Gregory R. Staats (*PBJ*, 89); he quotes *blues* lyrics to illustrate each meaning. 'Tight Like This' is a number by Armstrong's Savoy Ballroom Five (Okeh, 1928), in which Don Redman's ludicrous falsetto interjections leave the listener in no doubt that the former meaning is intended.

time The vast majority of jazz compositions are in common 4/4 *time*. Even 3/4 was often viewed as an aberration until the early 1960s: Norman Granz, contributing the sleevenote to Oscar Peterson's *Affinity* (Verve, 1962), noted that Peterson had 'taken waltzes, which formerly were anathema to jazz, and turned them into proper jazz vehicles'. The most celebrated attempt to escape from the 4/4 norm was Dave Brubeck's *Time Out* (Columbia, 1961), which included the hit single – in 5/4 – 'Take Five': see *take*.

Tom The charge of being a 'Tom' or an 'Uncle Tom' – from the character in Harriet Beecher Stowe's *Uncle Tom's Cabin* – has been levelled at a number of successful black jazz musicians, such as Louis Armstrong and *Fats* Waller. Leonard Feather, while conceding that Armstrong in his populist mode 'as seen on TV, might be called a Tom', argues that in his more important roles as black American and as jazzman he 'would have nothing to do with discrimination, as his integrated bands made clear' (*From Satchmo to Miles*, 30).

tooter A suitably disparaging term for any unadmired *horn* player, particularly a trumpeter.

trad Short for 'traditional', *trad* is a debased form of *Dixieland* jazz which became surprisingly popular in Britain in the late 1950s and early 1960s, with commercial hit singles such as Chris Barber's 'Petite Fleur' (Nixa, 1959), Acker Bilk's 'Summer Set' (Columbia, 1960), The Temperance Seven's 'You're Driving Me Crazy' (Parlophone, 1961) and Kenny Ball's 'Midnight in Moscow' (Pye Jazz, 1961), among many others. It is usually characterised by bright tones and lumpen rhythm, and some of its performers adopted funny hats or other sartorial oddities.

Tram Nickname of Frankie Trumbauer (1902–56), the saxophonist and bandleader with whom *Bix* Beiderbecke worked in the late 1920s.

Trane For many listeners, the work of saxophonist John Coltrane (1926–67) represents a frontier of jazz. Born in the same year as *Miles* Davis, and only six years younger than Charlie Parker, Coltrane might have been a young star of the *bebop* generation; instead, his reputation only began to take shape in 1955 when he joined Davis's quintet. He appeared on many of the most significant recording dates of the next few years – notably with Davis, including the indispensable *Kind of Blue* (Columbia, 1959), and with Thelonious *Monk* – before forming his own quartet in 1961: this was notable for its relentless exploration of often minimalist themes, especially in the LP-length four-movement piece, *A Love Supreme* (Impulse, 1964), a work of great power and inventiveness only slightly compromised by a spell of monotonous vocal incantation. The rhapsodic spirituality of *A Love Supreme* nevertheless starts to hint at the dangers of sacrificing musical principles to values which are less tangible (and less manageable). When Coltrane died, Philip Larkin, whose jazz criticism could be wittily perceptive even at its most hostile, wrote an obituary, which the *Daily Telegraph* declined to publish, in which he paid ironic tribute to Coltrane's 'stature'. 'If he was boring,' wrote Larkin, 'he was enormously boring. If he was ugly, he was massively ugly. To squeak and gibber for 16 bars is nothing; Coltrane could do it for 16 minutes' (Larkin, 213). Even a more sympathetic listener, Geoff Dyer, notes of Coltrane's 'last phase': 'While Coltrane's concerns were becoming ever more religious his music for the most part presents a violent landscape filled with chaos and shrieks' (*PBJ*, 389).

trombone If each of the main instruments of jazz has a distinct personality, then the *trombone* is all too evidently the vulgar, clowning comedian: *New Orleans* and *Dixieland* bands – and their *revivalist* imitators – found the instrument's farting slide-effects irresistible. 'Of all the instruments in the jazz fold,' says Humphrey Lyttelton, 'the trombone seems to have experienced the greatest difficulty in living down its past' (Lyttelton [2], 157). The *tailgate* trombone of *Kid* Ory provides the best examples of its use as a *front-line* instrument in New Orleans jazz. It also had an important supporting role in early jazz, providing harmonic colour and a bass line at a time when the string bass proved inaudible (especially on acoustic recordings) and the tuba impossibly cumbersome.

The trombone really only began to flourish as a serious jazz instrument once liberated from the New Orleans context. In Chicago, musicians such as Tommy Dorsey and Jack Teagarden extended its emotional range sometimes to the point of sentimentality; while in New York Joe 'Tricky Sam' Nanton and Lawrence Brown made it part of *Duke* Ellington's distinctive sound-picture. During the *swing* era, through the work of people like Vic Dickenson and Benny Morton, the trombone began to assume the role it subsequently made its own as the ideal ruminative and ironic foil for the alto or tenor sax: as it is, for instance, in the lovely 1950s collaborations of valve-trombonist Bob Brookmeyer with tenor player Stan Getz.

trumpet It often seems as if the *trumpet* (which here, as is customary, includes the *cornet*) has had all the *clarinet*'s luck. They are not, after all, so dissimilar in range or potential influence, yet in almost every jazz generation a trumpeter turns out to be the defining figure: Buddy Bolden, King Oliver, Louis Armstrong, Dizzy Gillespie, Miles Davis, Freddie Hubbard, Wynton Marsalis. Most of these musicians are mentioned in more detail elsewhere, so here it need only be remarked that a history of jazz without 'Potato Head Blues' is as unthinkable as one without *Kind of Blue*, and that the trumpet's range – from the golden open tone of *Satchmo* at his most commanding to the strangled whimper of *Miles* at his most introspective – is unequalled among other *front-line* instruments.

As that contrast suggests, the trumpet's different textures most clearly delineate the *hot* and the *cool* in jazz; Philip Larkin of course had the former in mind when he wrote, in 'Reasons for Attendance' of 'The trumpet's voice, loud and authoritative' (*Collected Poems*, 80).

James Campbell explains the enomously fashionable interest in jazz which developed in post-war Paris in the striking sentence: 'The solo trumpeter was the existentialist credo made flesh' (*PBJ*, 5). The jazz musician, he adds, 'improvising his freedom nightly, his notations a personal poetics of *Angst*, was a "man-simply-is" *par excellence*'. In *Look Back in Anger*, which received its first performance in May 1956, John Osborne appropriately makes his *angst*-ridden central character Jimmy Porter a jazz trumpeter. The play also contains, in the opening stage directions for Act II, a good example of a quite widespread misusage: 'In the room across the hall, Jimmy is playing on his

jazz trumpet, in intermittent bursts' (*Look Back in Anger*, 39).
What Osborne means, of course, is 'Jimmy is playing jazz on his
trumpet', and in practice he would have been better off without
'on his' altogether, since 'playing jazz trumpet' is always understood to mean 'playing jazz on the trumpet'; as it is, he has
invented an instrument which does not exist.

tuba Logically, the *tuba* should belong to jazz's pre-history – it
is part of the brass band heritage and, unlike the string *bass*,
can be carried and played by street-marching musicians – but
it survived mainly because it recorded audibly on the acoustic
system; it was quite rapidly superseded by the string bass after
the introduction of electric recording in 1926.

Tuxedo Band Oscar 'Papa' Celestin formed the Original
Tuxedo Orchestra in 1910 and, a year later, the Tuxedo Brass
Band, which was one of the leading *New Orleans* bands of its
time, especially notable for the number of subsequently
recorded jazz musicians – such as John Lindsay, Jimmy Noone
and Johnny St Cyr – among its members. Celestin's orchestra
'opened the Tuxedo Dance Hall in Storyville in 1910, and after
a gun fight at the Tuxedo Bar in 1913, where five men were shot
to death, he and his orchestra were out of work' (Tirro, 159).

two-handed A *two-handed* pianist is one who makes full and
equal use of his left hand, essentially for bass support but also
when appropriate for harmonic or melodic contributions, rather
than concentrating with his right hand on the instrument's upper
ranges: Oscar Peterson's 'two-handed style is muscular and
inventive' (Clarke, 333).

Ukulele   A miniature version of the *banjo*, more often employed for comic than for musical effect: the word is Hawaiian for 'jumping flea' (Chambers).

Uptown Lowdown   The short-lived *swing* era successor to *Delmonico's* in New York, 'The Uptown Lowdown put on a big floor show every night' but 'after two or three weeks the Updown Lowdown was down and out' (Max Kaminsky, *My Life in Jazz*, 76).

Vamp   A fill-in between choruses, usually of four bars, rather in the nature of a mid-performance *intro*.

Vanguard   New York based record label notable for distinguished 1950s *mainstream* recordings supervised by John Hammond and featuring such artists as Ruby Braff, Buck Clayton and Vic Dickenson.

Vendome   The Vendome Theatre in Chicago was especially noted in the late 1920s for the symphonic jazz performances of Erskine Tate and his orchestra which 'played hot music as well as overtures' (Louis Armstrong, quoted in Shapiro, 112).

Verve   The most successful of Norman Granz's labels, Verve was part of a jazz empire which also included Clef, Norgran and Jazz at the Philharmonic. It is hard to name a jazz performer of international stature who did *not* record for Verve in the 1950s (Armstrong, Ellington, Fitzgerald, Gillespie, Hawkins, Holliday, Parker, Tatum, Webster and Young are among those who did). Granz sold Verve to MGM in 1957, though he continued his association with it for some years before forming a new jazz label, Pablo.

vibes   'The vibraphone, like the xylophone,' remarks Leonard Feather, with commendable restraint, 'was an instrument long associated with novelty music' (*BOJ*, 134). There is indeed something inherently comical about the mallet-struck instruments, perhaps prompted by one's irreverent sense that fitting a keyboard might make things a great deal easier. Red Norvo was unique in jazz in making the xylophone his instrument for over twenty years, only switching to a form of vibraphone in 1943. The *vibes*, however, are more usually associated with Lionel Hampton and – above all – Milt Jackson, who in his work with the Modern Jazz Quartet finally overcame the instrument's irritating tendency to resemble a row of tinkling bottles overlaid with a hungover haze of vibrato. It is significant, of course, that the *MJQ* contains no wind instruments: the vibes work best in this somewhat austere and cerebral company of piano, bass and drums.

One particular appearance of the vibes should be noted, since it is one of the oddest moments in recorded jazz. The album *Monk's Music* (Riverside, 1957) whimsically opens with a brief (0'51") performance of 'Abide with Me', arranged by

Thelonious Monk for four horns without rhythm section; at the
end of bar 10, a passing-note is firmly and unmistakably struck
on a vibraphone, presumably by Monk himself, though it makes
no further appearance in the session and is unlisted in the
recording details. I know of no comparable occasion on which
an instrument – let alone such a comparatively exotic one as this
– is called upon to produce only a single note in an entire session.

Village Vanguard A long-established New York jazz club, especially famous for its Sunday matinées and, in the 1970s, for
hosting the comeback dates of performers such as Dexter
Gordon and Art Pepper.

violin With very few exceptions, the *violin* was rapidly displaced
in jazz by the more forceful reeds, and it became hard to take it
entirely seriously: it is the second instrument of Ellington trumpeter Ray Nance, but his digressions on it usually have a distinct
air of *hokum*. 'The violin, when it appeared in the early jazz
bands, was logically enough the maestro's instrument,' says John
Steiner (Hentoff, 153); this in itself contributed to its use more
for gesture than for performance.

viper 'It was that flashy, sawed-off runt of a jockey named
Patrick who made a viper out of me after Leon Rappolo failed,'
wrote *Mezz* Mezzrow in *Really the Blues* (*PBJ*, 142); a viper was
a marijuana smoker, and *Fats* Waller's title 'Viper's Drag' seems
thus to embody a nice pun.

Vocalion In the years up to the Second World War, the
American Vocalion company made pioneering records ranging
from Louis Armstrong through *Duke* Ellington to a pseudony-
mous *Count* Basie, billed as Jones-Smith Incorporated. In the
UK this legendary jazz label has been reactivated three times by
Decca: as a 78 rpm *New Orleans*-focused reissue series in the
1950s; as an alphabetically convenient substitute for *Vogue* in
the 1960s; and as an ambitiously-launched LP reissue series
(which seems, however, to have managed only four releases) in
the 1970s.

Vogue French jazz label licensed in the 1950s to UK Decca,
who developed it as an important umbrella outlet for American
jazz labels including Contemporary, Fantasy, Good Time Jazz
and Pacific Jazz/World Pacific; licensed to Pye from 1963
onwards. Is there a reason why jazz record producers (see also

Vanguard, Verve, Vocalion above) are peculiarly attracted to the letter V?

vout A form of *hip* nonsense-slang invented in the 1940s by Slim Gaillard and immortalised in the tracks he recorded with a band including Charlie Parker and Dizzy Gillespie (Bel Tone, 1945): one, 'Slim's Jam', has a good range of *vout*-speak while another, 'Flat Foot Floogie', was a huge commercial success. After that, according to *The Hip*, Gaillard 'was the man of the moment', running a restaurant 'which sold his own Vout City Beer' and peddling 'his legendary Vout City Dictionary for just a quarter' (Carr, 18). 'McVouty' was (usually) Jack McVea, tenor player in the 1945 band, though the prefix 'Mc', like the words 'vout' and *orooni*, could be applied at random to anyone or anything.

Wah-wah   A self-explanatory name for the muted trumpet style developed by Bubber Miley in his years with the *Duke* Ellington orchestra (1924–9) and incorporated in many Ellington arrangements: 'They were playing wah-wah music with plungers and things' (Louis Metcalf, quoted in Shapiro, 231).

walking   A *walking* rhythm is 'a moving, four-beat rhythmic pattern, usually said of the bass line' (Ulanov, 97).

washboard   This homely implement, which survived as a *rhythm* instrument in *skiffle*, has no place in developed jazz; it did, however, figure in *jug* bands and, in a rather ghostly way, on various records of the 1920s to which it was presumably thought to add a suitably 'authentic' air. Jim Godbolt points out that a number of early Parlophone jazz issues were credited to 'Louis Armstrong and his Washboard Beaters', though not all feature Armstrong and none contains a *washboard* (Ellington's 'Black and Tan Fantasy' seems to have been labelled thus); '"Armstrong and his Washboard Beaters" as a name to stick on the labels seemed to exert a peculiar fascination for one of the Parlophone executives' (Godbolt, 43).

There were washboard players in the country blues, one of whom, Washboard Sam (Robert Brown), also achieved a reputation as a blues singer; he recorded for Vocalion and, with his half-brother Big Bill Broonzy, for Bluebird.

Washingtonians   The Washingtonians were *Duke* Ellington's first band, formed in 1922, after Ellington and his Washington friends Otto Hardwick and Sonny Green arrived in New York.

wax   Originally, the wax master onto which, before the use of magnetic tape, a recorded performance was cut: hence, *to wax* is to record a number, and the finished *take* is a *waxing*: 'The highspot here is Johnny Hodges' first appearance on wax' (Larkin, 238).

West Coast   Geographical terms for jazz styles began to lose any precise meaning quite early on – by no means all *New Orleans* jazz came from the *crescent city*, and there were Chicagoans far from *Chicago* – so the 1950s designation *West Coast Jazz* looks like an anachronism or perhaps a convenient marketing tag with which Los Angeles-based labels like Capitol, Contemporary and Pacific could promote their *cool* jazz.

Nevertheless, from the late 1940s onwards 'Central Avenue, Los Angeles, became the Harlem of the West Coast' (Carr, 73): key figures included Chet Baker, Shelly Manne, Gerry Mulligan, Art Pepper and Shorty Rogers, while for many people an abiding image of West Coast cool remains Jimmy Giuffre's performance of 'The Train and the River' in the 1959 film *Jazz on a Summer's Day*. In an article about Giuffre first published in 1957, Whitney Balliett described him as 'one of the founders of the now declining West Coast school of modern jazz' which 'produced, in the main, a glazed, dainty small-band jazz' (*The Sound of Surprise*, 39).

Although Donald Clarke argues that West Coast jazz was 'largely a media invention which had the important side-effect of ignoring its black participants', he goes on to provide a definition which neatly encapsulates the qualities which made so many jazz critics nervous about the style: 'it was not pretentious or dramatic; what it was about was beauty... It swung and it was often lovely, but the frenetic quality of bop was largely gone' (Clarke, 318). For exactly the same reasons, it was that rarity in post-war jazz – a style which attracted a new popular audience without sacrificing musical intelligence.

West End The West End, or Bucktown, is a resort area on Lake Ponchartrain to the NW of *New Orleans*, which gave its name to *King* Oliver's composition 'West End Blues'. The celebrated recording of this piece by Louis Armstrong and his Hot Five (Okeh, 1928) has been described as 'immortal and perfect' (*JOR* [1], 16) and 'the most beautiful jazz record ever made' (Panassié, 274). The British issue launched Parlophone's 'New Rhythm Style Series' (R 448) in November 1929, though it was ironically labelled 'No.2', with 'Freeze an' Melt' by Eddie Lang's Orchestra on the other side billed as 'No.1'. Nevertheless, it remained in the catalogue until the last 78s were deleted, by which time it had been transferred to LP; 'West End Blues' thus has the distinction, rare for any recorded work, of having been continuously available for almost seventy years.

George Melly recalls that the first long engagement for Mick Mulligan's band was at the West End Café in Edinburgh: 'Even the name of the café, in appearance a conventional Scottish tearoom, was the same as a venue in Chicago where Armstrong had played in the early twenties' (*Owning-Up*, 77).

Wolverines A *Chicago*-based band, whose personnel in 1924 included two musicians who were to become legendary in rather different ways – the cornetist *Bix* Beiderbecke and the trombonist Tommy Dorsey; 'Wolverine Blues' was composed by *Jelly Roll* Morton in 1920. The wolverine is 'the American glutton: its fur. [Extension of *wolf*]' (Chambers).

woodshedding   '"Woodshedding" refers to practicing or rehearsing in private to gain technical mastery of one's instrument before going into a jam session' (Tirro, 217).

Woody'n You   A 'milestone' is how Ira Gitler describes 'Woody'n You', the piece *Dizzy* Gillespie contributed to a Coleman Hawkins session on 16 February 1944 which was 'the forst formal statement of the new music on record' (Gitler, 122): it was named for Woody Herman, who never recorded it – but Gillespie himself did on several occasions, including a big band version on which it is retitled 'Algo Bueno' (RCA Victor, 1947) and a later one with a fine small group (Verve, 1959).

work song   The *work song* – like the *blues* and the *spiritual* – was one of the major Afro-American formative components of jazz: 'Certain types of functional songs were... brought over by the slaves: "field hollers" and work songs in general, satirical songs and the like' (Newton, 30). Work songs, unlike spirituals, were both secular and practical: 'The function of the work song, as the name indicates, is purely utilitarian – to co-ordinate the efforts of the workers' (Stearns, 69). These workers, of course, were forced labourers, often in chain gangs: consequently, the work song survived mainly in the prison farms of the southern USA, where it was researched and recorded by specialists such as Alan Lomax. Its echoes remain, in the more soulful or *funky* aspects of modern jazz – in pieces like Nat Adderley's 'Work Song' (Riverside, 1960) or Bobby Timmons' 'Moanin"' (Riverside, 1961) – and in Sam Cooke's commercially successful song 'Chain Gang' (RCA Victor, 1960).

X In the early 1950s, the bootleg 'Label X' reissued early rare jazz 78s on LP until sued by RCA, who then discovered that the pirate discs had been pressed in their own factory. Subsequently, Orrin Keepnews and Bill Grauer, founders of *Riverside* records, 'programmed a series of suggested official RCA reissue albums ... which came out as ten-inch LPs released on RCA's "X" label' (Priestley, 101).

xylophone Seldom used in jazz, the *xylophone* was nevertheless Red Norvo's instrument until he switched in 1943 to the *vibes*; Leonard Feather describes it as 'a sort of dehydrated vibraphone' (*BOJ*, 133).

Yardbird The nickname of Charlie Parker, usually shortened to *Bird*.

Yazoo The Yazoo river joins the *Mississippi* at Vicksburg; between them, stretching up to *Memphis*, lies the Mississippi *Delta*, the heartland of the country *blues*.

Yerba Buena Band A 'vigorous and brash jazz group' (*JOR* [1], 329) of *revivalist* musicians, based on the format of *King* Oliver's Creole Jazz Band, founded by Lu Watters in 1940: they recorded copiously for the Hollywood-based Good Time Jazz label, and their blend of enthusiasm and over-emphasis is characteristic of the *New Orleans* revival of the 1940s.

Zoot   A *zoot suit* is 'a flashy type of man's suit with padded shoulders, fitted waist, knee-length coat, and trousers narrow at the ankles (introduced late 1940s)' (Chambers). The saxophonist Zoot Sims is one of the least obtrusively influential figures in *modern* jazz: after playing with the Woody Herman and Stan Kenton bands in the late 1940s, he went on to work with a wide range of smaller groups and – as *Jazz on Record* puts it – his 'recorded output is of such a consistently high quality that the collector can buy "blind" (or perhaps "deaf") and be sure of satisfaction' (*JOR* [1], 280).

Bibliography

This bibliography includes books on jazz and a few other reference works which are cited on several occasions in the text; it does *not* list other books less frequently mentioned nor items in magazines and newspapers. References are to the first edition except where a second or subsequent edition is also listed in this Bibliography. If I have used an abbreviated form for citations, this is noted in brackets.

Balliett, Whitney: *The Sound of Surprise*. London: William Kimber, 1960; Harmondsworth: Pelican, 1963.

Balliett, Whitney: *Dinosaurs in the Morning*. London: Phoenix House, 1962.

Berendt, Joachim: *The New Jazz Book*. London: Jazz Book Club, 1965. (Berendt)

Campbell, James (ed): *The Picador Book of Blues and Jazz*. London: Picador, 1995. (*PBJ*)

Carr, Roy, and Brian Case, Fred Dellar: *The Hip*. London: Faber, 1986. (Carr)

Clarke, Donald: *The Rise and Fall of Popular Music*. London: Penguin, 1995. (Clarke)

Clayton, Peter and Peter Gammond: *Jazz A–Z*. Enfield: Guinness Books, 1986.

de Toledano, Ralph (ed): *Frontiers of Jazz*. London: Jazz Book Club, 1966. (de Toledano)

Feather, Leonard: *The Book of Jazz*. New York: Meridian Books, 1959. (*BOJ*)

Feather, Leonard: *From Satchmo to Miles*. London: Quartet Books, 1972.

Fox, Charles, and Peter Gammond, Alun Morgan, Alexis Korner: *Jazz on Record: A Critical Guide*. London: Arrow Books, 1960. (*JOR* [1])

Gitler, Ira: *Swing to Bop*. New York: Oxford University Press, 1985. (Gitler)

Godbolt, Jim: *A History of Jazz in Britain 1919-50*. London: Quartet Books, 1984. (Godbolt)

Green, Jonathon: *The Dictionary of Contemporary Slang*. London:

144

Pan, 1984. (Green)

Hardy, Phil and Dave Laing: *The Faber Companion to 20th Century Popular Music*. London: Faber, 1990. (Hardy)

Harris, Rex: *Jazz*. Harmondsworth: Pelican, 1952. (Harris)

Harrison, Max: *A Jazz Retrospect*. Newton Abbot: David & Charles, 1976. (Harrison)

Hentoff, Nat and Albert McCarthy (eds): *Jazz*. London: Cassell, 1959. (Hentoff)

Hodeir, André: *Toward Jazz*. New York: Grove Press, 1962.

Kaminsky, Max: *My Life in Jazz*. London: André Deutsch, 1963.

Larkin, Philip: *All What Jazz?* London: Faber, 1970. (Larkin)

Lyttelton, Humphrey: *The Best of Jazz: Basin Street to Harlem*. London: Robson Books, 1978; Harmondsworth: Penguin, 1980. (Lyttelton [1])

Lyttelton, Humphrey: *The Best of Jazz: Enter the Giants*. London: Robson Books, 1981; London: Unwin Paperbacks, 1984. (Lyttelton [2])

McCarthy, Albert (ed): *The PL Yearbook of Jazz*. London: Editions Poetry London, 1946. (McCarthy)

McCarthy, Albert, and Alun Morgan, Paul Oliver, Max Harrison: *Jazz on Record: A Critical Guide*. London: Hanover Books, 1968. (JOR [2])

Melly, George: *Owning-Up*. London: Weidenfeld & Nicolson, 1965; Harmondsworth: Penguin, 1970.

Newton, Francis: *The Jazz Scene*. London: MacGibbon & Kee, 1959; Harmondsworth: Penguin, 1961. (Newton)

Panassié, Hugues and Madeleine Gautier: *Dictionary of Jazz*. London: Jazz Book Club, 1959. (Panassié)

Priestley, Brian: *Jazz on Record: A History*. London: Elm Tree Books, 1988. (Priestley)

Reisner, Robert George: *Bird: The Legend of Charlie Parker*. New York: Citadel Press, 1962.

Scholes, Percy A.: *The Oxford Companion to Music*, Ninth Edition. London: Oxford University Press, 1955. (Scholes)

Shapiro, Nat, and Nat Hentoff: *Hear Me Talkin' to Ya*. London: Peter Davies, 1955; Harmondsworth: Penguin, 1962. (Shapiro)

Stearns, Marshall: *The Story of Jazz*. New York: Oxford University Press, 1956; New York: Mentor Books, 1958. (Stearns)

Tirro, Frank: *Jazz: A History*. London: Dent, 1979. (Tirro)

Ulanov, Barry: *A Handbook of Jazz*. London: Hutchinson,

1958. (Ulanov)
Williams, Martin: *The Jazz Tradition*. New York: Oxford
University Press, 1993. (Williams)

I am grateful to Scorpio Books, 1 Nethergate Street, Bungay,
Suffolk NR35 1HE (telephone 01986 895743) – somewhat
improbably, a secondhand bookshop in the middle of East Anglia
which specialises in jazz – for supplying me with several of the
out-of-print books listed above.

Listening to Jazz

Many books on jazz include lists of ten, twenty or a hundred essential recordings, an exercise which, apart from enabling an author a chance to choose his 'Desert Island Discs', seldom serves much purpose since in most cases the reader will have had a knowledgeable interest in jazz before he picked up the book in the first place. But I have in mind another reader, possibly as hypothetical as the Yeatsian fisherman, who has come to this particular book primarily through an interest in language or in the series to which it belongs and who may remain sceptical about the claims jazz might make on his or her attention. The musical allegiances of this reader – like those of this writer – are essentially rooted in the European classical tradition: he or she detests the noisy ubiquity of pop and rock music, is deeply suspicious of fusions and crossovers, and is moved to set-endangering fury by the sudden eruptions of cabaret music or indeed jazz in the early evening programme on Radio 3. So am I. Jazz is not a poor relation of classical music, to be called upon to fill an awkward gap or reduce the stress of 'drive-time': it demands, if not different ears, then at least a distinct and equal kind of attentive respect.

So, for that notional reader who has come this far with me but who isn't at all sure about the music itself, here are some fairly arbitrary suggestions. They exclude the early years (pre-1925) which may at first strike you as impossibly primitive in recording if not in execution and the recent period (post-1975) in which jazz is doing diverse things which may obscure its essential characteristics: try them later. They also exclude singers, even though I would want both Ella Fitzgerald and Billie Holiday on my desert island and could readily have allowed them to figure overwhelmingly in my choices, because at its centre jazz is an instrumental music, though shading into the vocal blues on one side and popular song on the other. This, then, is absolutely not a definitive list but a modest selection of thirty tracks – many of them cited in the text of this book – which I might play to someone who wanted to know what jazz is about: if at least half of them don't delight and astonish you, then you almost

147

certainly don't like jazz.

1. Fletcher Henderson & His Orchestra: 'Hot Mustard' (Brunswick, 1926)
2. Louis Armstrong & His Hot Seven: 'Potato Head Blues' (Okeh, 1927)
3. Duke Ellington & His Orchestra: 'Black and Tan Fantasy' (Okeh, 1927)
4. Louis Armstrong and Earl Hines: 'Weather Bird' (Okeh, 1928)
5. Louis Armstrong & His Orchestra: 'St Louis Blues' (Okeh, 1929)
6. Duke Ellington & His Famous Orchestra: 'It Don't Mean a Thing (if it ain't got that swing)' (Brunswick, 1932)
7. Jelly Roll Morton: 'Buddy Bolden's Blues' (Commodore, 1939)
8. Sidney Bechet & His New Orleans Feetwarmers: 'Shake It and Break It' (RCA Victor, 1940)
9. Duke Ellington & His Orchestra: 'All Too Soon' (RCA Victor, 1940)
10. Duke Ellington & His Orchestra: 'In a Mellotone' (RCA Victor, 1940)
11. Coleman Hawkins & Leonard Feather's All Stars: 'Mop-Mop' (Commodore, 1943)
12. Lester Young Quintet: 'Blue Lester' (Savoy, 1944)
13. Charlie Parker Septet: 'Ornithology' (Dial, 1946)
14. Charlie Parker Quintet: 'Embraceable You' (Dial, 1947)
15. Bud Powell Trio: 'Indiana' (Roost, 1947)
16. Charlie Parker All Stars: 'Parker's Mood' (Savoy, 1948)
17. Miles Davis Nonet: 'Jeru' (Capitol, 1949)
18. Thelonious Monk Quintet: 'Smoke Gets in Your Eyes' (Prestige, 1954)
19. Modern Jazz Quartet: 'Django' (Prestige, 1954)
20. Bill Evans Trio: 'Easy Living' (Riverside, 1956)
21. Thelonious Monk: 'Round Midnight' (Riverside, 1957)
22. Thelonious Monk Septet: 'Well, You Needn't' (Riverside, 1957)
23. Coleman Hawkins Quintet: 'My One and Only Love' (Felsted, 1958)
24. Dizzy Gillespie Quintet: 'Woody 'n You' (Verve, 1959)
25. Miles Davis Sextet: 'So What' (Columbia, 1959)
26. Art Blakey & The Jazz Messengers: 'Blue Moon' (United Artists, 1962)
27. John Coltrane Quartet: 'A Love Supreme' (Impulse, 1964)

28. Clarke-Boland Big Band: 'Reprieve' (Black Lion, 1969)
29. Earl Hines: 'Blue Sands' (Black Lion, 1972)
30. Duke Ellington Quartet: 'Prelude to a Kiss' (Pablo, 1973)

Discographical Note

Recordings are, even more than books, the primary resource for anyone interested in jazz – and a number of important ones are consequently cited in the text. To include full discographical details, however, would entail listing more numbers than a phone book, with the additional irritation of many being unhelpfully out of date. Although jazz is astonishingly fortunate in possessing this historical documentation, its accessibility is complicated by two factors. Firstly, the past fifty years have seen two complete changes of format – from 78 to LP, and from LP to CD – each with its attendant cycle of deletion followed by reissue, repackaging, reshuffling, relabelling. Secondly, and even more significantly, the transatlantic licensing arrangements of jazz record companies have been quite extraordinarily complicated.

The problem is most acute with the smaller labels: for example, Savoy – with its indispensable 1940s recordings of Gillespie, Parker, Young and so on – has to my knowledge been licensed since then in the UK to Melodisc, Decca/London, ARC/Eros, Oriole/Realm, CBS, Arista, RCA/Ariola and probably to others as well. With bootleg recordings or labels which vanished into obscurity, such as Guild/Musicraft, the problems are compounded: hence, the occasional startling appearance of major performances in tackily-packaged budget-price reissues on supermarkets' and newsagents' racks. And, of course, the recordings of jazz's earlier years are now out of copyright altogether and can be re-released by anyone, competent or not.

The major record companies look more straightfoward but conceal a particularly fiendish trap for the unwary in the way that American and British owners of identical trademarks became divorced from each other. Thus, Victor (later RCA Victor), with its portrait of the attentive dog Nipper, was wedded to the similarly-identified HMV only until 1957; Columbia, and its 'magic notes', parted company with its English counterpart in 1953, to be re-united (under the Japanese ownership of Sony) thirty years later; American Decca was established in 1934 as a branch of the similarly-named English company, but its products were marketed by UK Decca as Brunswick (by the 1950s this had evolved into a sophisticated game of transatlantic musical chairs played with the trademarks Decca, Brunswick, Coral, London and Vocalion). A perverse and wonderful exception is Okeh which, though owned by American Columbia since 1926, has almost always been licensed to Parlophone. Brian Priestley's *Jazz on Record: A History* offers some signposts through this minefield, as do two earlier books called *Jazz on Record* by Fox *et al* and McCarthy *et al*.

In these somewhat confusing circumstances, which are part of the fun for collectors and maddening for anyone else, I have attempted to provide record citations with a parenthetical note of the original, usually by definition American, issue – e.g. (Okeh, 1928) or (Dial, 1947).

*

The solution to the crossword clue quoted under *cakewalk* is: Abundance.